THE CRY TO GOD IN THE OLD TESTAMENT

SOCIETY
OF BIBLICAL
LITERATURE

DISSERTATION SERIES
J. J. M. Roberts, Old Testament Editor
Charles Talbert, New Testament Editor

Number 103

THE CRY TO GOD
IN THE OLD TESTAMENT

by
Richard Nelson Boyce

Richard Nelson Boyce

THE CRY TO GOD
IN THE OLD TESTAMENT

Scholars Press
Atlanta, Georgia

THE CRY TO GOD
IN THE OLD TESTAMENT

Richard Nelson Boyce

Ph.D., 1985
Union Theological Seminary in Virginia

Advisor:
James L. Mays

© 1988
Society of Biblical Literature

Library of Congress Cataloging-in-Publication Data

Boyce, Richard Nelson.
  The cry to God in the Old Testament.

  (Dissertation series / Society of Biblical
Literature ; no. 103)
  Bibliography: p.
  1. Laments in the Bible. 2. Bible. O.T. – Criticism,
interpretation, etc. I. Title. II. Series:
Dissertation series (Society of Biblical Literature);
no. 103.
BS1199.L27B69 1988   221.6   88-4589
ISBN 1-55540-229-1 (alk. paper)
ISBN 1-55540-230-5 (pbk. : alk. paper)

Printed in the United States of America

Contents

Acknowledgments

This space is dedicated to the acknowledgment of three types of assistance integral to the initiation, progress, and completion of this dissertation.

For inspiration, encouragement, and guidance. Here I thank the members of my dissertation committee: Dr. Patrick D. Miller, Jr.—for my initial interest in the "cry" and the passion for words and language from which this interest grew; Dr. James L. Mays—for adopting a project half-complete and for the vision necessary to forge the parts into a whole; and Dr. W. Sibley Towner—for setting the project in perspective and challenging me to be careful yet bold.

For support along the way. Here I thank the Session of Lakeside Presbyterian Church, Richmond, Virginia, for their generous and tangible assistance in this endeavor and Sally Hicks and Martha B. Aycock of Union Seminary for the skill and care with which they converted an often unruly manuscript into proper black and white.

For the vision of the end. Here I thank my wife, Kathleen, who kept me moving forward, keeping before me the dreams we had both delayed in order to see this smaller dream to fruition.

It is to be understood that these acknowledgments in no way excuse any absence of passion, care, or vision on my part. They simply seek to make clear that when such qualities are occasionally present they are by no means the creations of one person alone.

List of Illustrations

List of Abbreviations

ANET	*Ancient Near Eastern Texts Relating to the Old Testament*
BDB	*A Hebrew and English Lexicon of the Old Testament*
D.O.	direct object
Dtr	deuteronomic
DtrH	Deuteronomistic History
E	Elohistic
hif	hiphil stem
hitp	hithpael stem
hitpol	hithpolel stem
I.O.	indirect object
J	Yahwistic
LXX	The Septuagint
MT	The Masoretic Text
nif	niphal stem
P	Priestly
pi	piel stem
TDOT	*Theological Dictionary of the Old Testament*
THAT	*Theologisches Handwörterbuch zum Alten Testament*

All translations of Scripture are my own.
Versification follows that of the Hebrew text.

1
Introduction

"Then we cried to the Lord
the God of our fathers, . . ."
— Deut 26:7a

In a fundamental sense, the Old Testament is a story of a relationship — a relationship rooted in the crying out of God's people on the one hand and God's hearing of these cries on the other. This vocally-grounded relationship is so basic to the message of the Old Testament as a whole that the two-fold construct of humankind's cry of distress and God's saving hearing has left its mark on the most varied of materials, ranging from the stipulations of its legal codes (Exod 22:22) to the proverbs of its wisdom materials (Prov 21:13). At the beginning of the primeval history, one encounters the crying and hearinq of Abel's blood (Gen 4:10); at the end of salvation history, the prophet Isaiah envisions the cessation of the cry (Isa 65:19). In between, at numerous points, the crying out of the people of Israel and the saving response of their God Yahweh serves as a "red thread" binding together the history of this God with this people (e.g., Exod 3:7, 9; 14:10, 15; Num 11:2; Judg 3:9, 15; 1 Sam 12:8, 10)[1]

Given the comprehensive nature of this two-fold construct, its specificity with respect to vocabulary and form is remarkable. This is especially true when the writers of the Old Testament use this pattern to look back on the history of God's relationship with their predecessors in the faith. Whether included within a request sent to a king (Num 20:16), an offering of one's first fruits (Deut 26:7), a service of covenant renewal (Josh 24:7), a liturgy of communal lamentation (Neh 9:27), or less easily placed laments of the individual (Ps 22:6) and praises of the people (Ps 107:6, 13, 19, 28), the terminology and pattern are quite consistent. Some person or persons in Israel's collective past cried out in the direction of God (in all the preceding examples, z^cq or s^cq with the directional

---

[1] See R. Albertz, "s^cq, schreien," in *Theologisches Handwörterbuch zum Alten Testament*, hrsg. von E. Jenni unter Mitarbeit von C. Westermann (München: Chr. Kaiser Verlag, 971), II:574; and G. Hasel, "$zā^caq$," in *Theological Dictionary of the Old Testament*, ed. by G. J. Botterweck and H. Ringgren, trans. by D. E. Green (Grand Rapids: William B. Eerdmans Publishing Co., 1980), IV:120–21. These two wordbooks hereafter referred to as *THAT* and *TDOT* respectively.

preposition *'el*) following which God responded with various acts of salvation (characterized by such words as *yš'* — nif and hif; *nsl* — nif and hif; and *ys'* — hif).

Considering this surprising combination of specificity and comprehensiveness, two trends in today's use of the biblical cry of distress are striking: (1) its uncritical use in some areas of modern theology (especially those broadly defined as theologies of "liberation"); and (2) the lack of its use in others (particularly in recent writings dealing with the subject of prayer).

With regard to the first trend, the popularity of this theme of the "cry" becomes obvious even through a cursory glance at book titles. For example, the October 1984 issue of the magazine *Sojourners* lists such titles as *The Cry of My People: Out of Captivity in Latin America* and *Cry of the People* within a group of recent books under the heading "Liberation: The Cry of the Poor."[2] Persons well-read in this area might here supply their own comparable lists. However, even where such a focus on the cry occurs on a more scholarly level, accompanied by a perceptive and sensitive handling of specific biblical texts, the semantics and function of the cry itself are left on a level of meaning so general as to leave it open to the most varied, if not conflicting, social, political, and theological interpretations. This is true even of J. P. Miranda who, in his book *Marx and the Bible,* while citing the "technical" nature of this term and linking its use in such passages as Exod 3:7, Gen 4:10, and Exod 22:21–23, nevertheless defines it quite generally as "the cry of the poor and the oppressed."[3]

With regard to the second trend, the lack of this theme of the "cry" in almost all the fairly scant modern wrestlings with a theology of prayer is even more distressing and may be linked with an anti-petitionary stance at their core. This discomfort with any theology of prayer grounded primarily in the attitude of petition can be demonstrated by quotes on both a "popular" and a more "scholarly" level. Harold S. Kushner, in a book in the "popular" vein, states:

> I am not sure that prayer puts us in touch with God the way many people think it does—that we approach God as a supplicant, a beggar asking for favors, or as a customer presenting Him with a shopping list and asking what it will cost. Prayer is not primarily a matter of asking God to change things. If we can come to understand what prayer can and should be, and rid ourselves of such unrealistic expectations, we will be better able to call on prayer, and on God, when we need them most.[4]

Gordon Kaufman, though addressing a more "scholarly" audience, ends a chapter on a similar note:

---

[2] "Sojourners Book Service," *Sojourners,* October 1984, pp. 32–33.

[3] J. P. Miranda, *Marx and the Bible: A Critique of the Philosophy of Oppression,* trans. by J. Eagleson (Maryknoll: Orbis Books, 1974), p. 95.

[4] Harold S. Kushner, *When Bad Things Happen to Good People* (New York: Avon, 1981), p. 122.

Christian piety has too long been nurtured largely on those psalms and other biblical materials which portray God as a kind of genie who will extricate the faithful from the difficulties into which they fall; it is this erratic and fickle God who cannot be reconciled with the modern understanding of the order in nature and history. Far better would it be to nourish our piety on the paradigmatic Christian story: a man praying that this cup might pass from him but submitting his will to God's, no matter what the consequences; that prayer answered not with legions of anqels to rescue him but with lonely suffering on a cross, culminating in a cry of despair before the moment of death—and then a resurrection of new life, new faith, new hope, new love, and a new community born after his death.[5]

Given this pattern of misuse and avoidance, this dissertation returns to the use of the "cry" which should be most basic for understanding—that of the Old Testament writers, editors, and compilers themselves. The primary focus of this study will be those two Hebrew words most consistently chosen within the biblical material itself when a "cry" was looked back on in a summary fashion (Num 20:16; Deut 26:7; etc.): the word-pair z'q/s'q and their nominal derivatives. It shall attempt to analyze as precisely as possible the semantics and function of these two words for vocalization by viewing them within three separate but interrelated contexts:

The Word Field. In chapter two, z'q and ṣ'q will be compared and contrasted with the host of Old Testament words for vocal activity of a similar nature. This will be done in order to specify these words' meaning and function as precisely as possible over against those of associated words which might have been chosen in their stead. This chapter will thus be an attempt to incorporate several of the "new" approaches to both biblical and nonbiblical word-studies (particularly that of "structural" semantics)[6] in a manner appropriate to the two principal words involved.

A Setting-in-Life. In chapter three, one particular setting-in-life will be analyzed in which a "directed" form (i.e., followed by the directional preposition *'el*) of one or the other of these words is consistently used. This will be done in

---

[5] Gordon D. Kaufman, *God the Problem* (Cambridge: Harvard University Press, 1972), p. 147.

[6] Several resources of a general nature are central to the "structural" emphasis of this particular chapter: John Lyons, *Introduction to Theoretical Linguistics* (Cambridge: University Press, 1968); Stephen Ullmann, *Semantics: An Introduction to the Science of Meaning* (New York: Barnes & Noble, 1962); and Moisés Silva, *Biblical Words and Their Meaning: An Introduction to Lexical Semantics* (Grand Rapids: Zondervan Publishing House, 1983). In addition, several studies of a more "applied" variety have been helpful: John F. A. Sawyer, *Semantics in Biblical Research: New Methods of Defining Hebrew Words for Salvation,* Studies in Biblical Theology, 2d ser., no. 24 (London: SCM Press, 1972); Samuel E. Ballentine, *The Hidden God: The Hiding of the Face of God in the Old Testament,* Oxford Theological Monographs (Oxford: University Press, 1983); and James Barr, "The Image of God in the Book of Genesis—A Study of Terminology," *Bulletin of John Rylands Library* 51 (1968–1969): 11–26.

order to specify as precisely as possible the semantics and function of this form of the cry in this and analogous situational contexts. The third chapter will thus be an attempt to recapture the early form-critics' appreciation of the importance of setting-in-life for meaning (especially as evidenced in the recent interest in the various "social" contexts of biblical language)[7] through an analysis of a particular social setting especially illuminating with respect to the two principal words at hand.

Setting in Literature. In chapter four, the various forms of that particular vocalization so central to the Old Testament story of God and his people—the cry of the slaves in Egypt—will be analyzed according to the varying literary traditions of which they are a part. This chapter will be an attempt to use the relevant tools of literary, form-critical, and redactional analysis (especially as exemplified by several recent scholars with regard to the material at hand)[8] in order to differentiate the underlying conceptual frameworks within which these various "cries" of the slaves must be understood. A question of "appropriation" will thus be central to both the method and the results of this chapter. How did the writers, editors, and compilers of the Old Testament traditions seek to appropriate the heard cries of their forebears through the selection of particular terms for these vocalizations and their placement in various settings in life and in literature?

---

[7] Particularly important in this regard was an initial interest sparked by a study of the life setting of selected vocabulary of the Old Testament laments by Patrick D. Miller, Jr., "Trouble and Woe: Interpreting the Biblical Laments," *Interpretation* 37 (January 1983) 32–45. Also significant for the progress of this chapter were extensive studies linking particular forms of speech, gestures, and ritual actions to various social contexts within the life of the Ancient Near East: Erhard S. Gerstenberger, *Der bittende Mensch: Bittritual und Klaglied des Einzelnen im Alten Testament,* Wissenschaftliche Monographien zum Alten und Neuen Testament, Bd. 51 (Neukirchen-Vluyn: Neukirchener Verlag, 1980); Moshe Greenberg, *Biblical Prose Prayer: As a Window to the Popular Religion of Ancient Israel,* The Taubman Lectures in Jewish Studies, 6th ser. (Berkeley: University of California Press, 1983); and Othmar Keel, *The Symbolism of the Biblical World: Ancient Near Eastern Iconography and the Book of Psalms,* trans. by Timothy J. Hallett (New York: The Seabury Press, 1978).

[8] Central to the development of this chapter is the work of various scholars on selected biblical material, especially the following: (a) on the Book of Exodus, Werner H. Schmidt, *Exodus,* Biblischer Kommentar Altes Testament, Bd. II/2 (Neukirchen-Vluyn: Neukirchener Verlag, 1977); James Plastaras, *The God of Exodus: The Theology of the Exodus Narratives* (Milwaukee: Bruce Publishing Company, 1966); and Brevard S. Childs, *The Book of Exodus: A Critical, Theological Commentary,* The Old Testament Library (Philadelphia: The Westminster Press, 1974); (b) on the Book of Genesis, Claus Westermann, *Genesis 1–11: A Commentary,* trans. by John J. Scullion (Minneapolis: Augsburg Publishing House, 1984); and (c) on the Deuteronomic formula in the Book of Judges, Walter Brueggemann, "Social Criticism and Social Vision in the Deuteronomic Formula of the Judges," in *Die Botschaft und die Boten: Festschrift für Hans Walter Wolff zum 70. Geburtstag,* hrsg. von Jörg Jeremias und Lothar Perlitt (Neukirchen-Vluyn: Neukirchener Verlag, 1981), pp. 101–114.

The concluding chapter of the dissertation will indicate several ways in which the patterns of the biblical appropriation of this "cry" could or should offer guidance with respect to similar attempts at appropriation today. In particular, guidelines will be offered for the proper appropriation of the biblical cry of distress in the areas of liberation theology and the theology of prayer. The chapter will close with a brief sketch of how such patterns for the appropriation of the cry may be traced in the New Testament portrayal of the saving work of Jesus Christ.

2
The Word Field

> The value of a word is first known when we mark it off against the value of neighboring and opposing words. Only as part of the whole does the word have sense; for only in the field is there meaning.
>
> J. Trier, *Der deutsch Wortschatz im Sinn-bezirk des Verstandes,* p. 6, translated and quoted in Silva, *Biblical Words,* p. 161.

Readers of English attribute meaning to the verb "cry" in the sentence, "then we cried to the Lord," in two ways: (1) they recognize the relations between this verb and the other words before and after it (subject and prepositional phrase) and derive meaning from these relations between words *within the sentence;* and (2) they recognize the relations between this verb and other words which might fill the same slot (synonyms, antonymns, hyponyms, etc.) and derive meaning from these relations between words *beyond the sentence.* The linguist identifies the former combinatory sense relations as "syntagmatic," the latter contrasting sense relations as "paradigmatic" (Silva, *Biblical Words,* p. 119.) Both attribute meaning not so much to a relation between a word and its referent (a "referential" approach to meaning), as to the relations between a word and the words of its lexical system (a "structural" approach to meaning). This approach is dictated by the nature of the English verb "cry." Because of the vast field of words in English associated with vocalization (e.g., "speak," "petition," "call," "scream," "shout") it is not the *word itself* which "signifies" in the sentence above; instead, it is the *choice* of this word rather than another from its field. (This principle is expounded in Barr, "The Image of God," p. 15.)

It is the premise of this chapter that readers of Hebrew should attribute meaning to the verb *ṣ'q* in the sentence *wanniṣ'aq 'el-yhwh 'ĕlōhê 'ăbōtênû* in a similar fashion. Here too meaning may be derived from the relations between this verb and other words or signs *within the sentence* (e.g., the inflected subject and the prepositional phrase), i.e., syntagmatic sense relations. Here too meaning may be derived from the relations between this verb and other words *beyond the sentence* (e.g., *qr', z'q, 'nḥ*-nif, *rnn, šw'*-pi), i.e., paradigmatic sense relations. As with the English verb "cry," this approach is dictated by the nature of the word involved (a verb for the wide-ranging activity of vocalization). Because of the

7

large number of biblical words for such vocal activity, meaning is viewed not so much as a relation between a word and its referent (in this case, the making of sounds with the vocal cords). Instead, the meaning of the Hebrew word $s'q$ is seen primarily as a function of "choices within the lexical stock of a given language at a given time" (Barr, "Image of God," p. 15).

The language and time for the lexical stock of this chapter's study is that supplied by the Masoretic text of the Hebrew Scriptures[1] The field of words to be examined are all the Hebrew verbs[2] which occur more than five times[3] and which may be related semantically to the activity of vocalization.[4] Using this vast field of "choices" available to the writer, recorder, or compiler of the Hebrew Scriptures, this chapter will attempt to describe the range of meanings signified by a "choice" of $z'q$ or $s'q$, regardless of the situational or literary context within which these words appear (the subjects of chapters 3 and 4). A final section will deal with the *particular* "choices" (both syntagmatic and paradigmatic) available to the writer, recorder, or compiler of the Hebrew Scriptures for specifying *particular* meanings of $z'q$ and $s'q$ within this broader range. Examples of the latter will close the chapter.

It should be noted at this point that for the purposes of this chapter, as well as the dissertation as a whole, any semantic distinction between the verbs $z'q$ and $s'q$ *themselves* is considered inconsequential. All "choices" between $z'q$ and $s'q$ within the Hebrew scriptures are therefore assumed to be purely orthographic.[5]

---

[1] This particular context for interpretation is similar to the "situational context" chosen by Sawyer in his study of Hebrew words for salvation (Sawyer, *Semantics in Biblical Research*, pp. 10–16). However, it should be noted that while this may be the proper context for the word field study of this chapter, it may not be for the chapters to follow (especially chapter four on the setting in literature).

[2] Though nominal forms of the verbs $z'q$ and $s'q$ will prove central to the "patterns" of later chapters, the priority of verbal forms for meaning is assumed for the analysis of this chapter. Particularly with regard to syntagmatic patterns, the process of nominalization makes an identical treatment of verbal and nominal forms inadvisable at this initial stage (cf. Sawyer, *Semantics*, pp. 63–69; and Silva, *Biblical Words*, p. 162n).

[3] Though this is an admittedly arbitrary number, the rationale for such a cutoff is quite straightforward: the major thrust of this dissertation has to do not with the "referent" of a host of narrowly attested Hebrew words, but the "sense" of a few widely attested and highly significant ones (cf. Silva, *Biblical Words*, pp. 100–117). With less than five citations, such delineation of "senses" is highly problematic and inappropriate for the prevailing methodology of this chapter.

[4] At this stage, the definition of the field is left as broad as possible. It does not limit either the maker or recipient of the sound to any particular class (human, animal, or divine). Nor does it restrict the sound itself to any level of articulation or intensity or purpose ("to summon," "to proclaim," "to call for help," etc.).

[5] There are some statistics which might tempt one to distinguish between the use of $z'q$ and $s'q$, e.g., the "preference" for $s'q$ in the Pentateuch (26 out of 27 times, Albertz, "$s'q$," *THAT* 2, 569) and a similar "preference" with regard to explicit "crying out" to *persons* versus *God* (11 out of 12 times, as listed in Francis Brown, S. R. Driver, and Charles A.

I. SYNTAGMATIC CUES TO MEANING

A study of the relations between words within biblical sentences employing
$z^c q$ or $s^c q$ reveals three essential syntagmatic patterns characteristic of their use:
(1) both these verbs occur in the majority of cases without a direct object;[6] (2)
if they have a direct object, it is limited to substantives or object clauses concerned with vocalization;[7] and (3) they cannot take an indirect object, but only an
object of the preposition.[8] These three essential syntagmatic patterns are ones
which $z^c q$ and $s^c q$ share with most of the words of the next section (exception
qr'),[9] which must thus be distinguished paradigmatically. These patterns are not,
however, ones shared by *all* Hebrew verbs associated with vocalization. In this
section, the syntagmatic patterns of $z^c q$ and $s^c q$ will therefore be contrasted with
the differing syntagmatic patterns of three groups of words from their field
(labeled "function," "process," and "action" verbs). Through this contrast, the

---

Briggs, eds., *A Hebrew and English Lexicon of the Old Testament* [Oxford: Clarendon
Press, 1909], pp. 277, 858; hereafter referred to as *BDB*). However, the apparent inter-
changeability of these words within various periods and textual groups as well as similar
dual forms in Aramaic, Arabic, and Samaritan argue against such distinctions (Hasel,
"*zā'aq*," *TDOT* 4, 114).

[6] Here reference is made only to these words' predominant use in the qal stem (107 of
128 occurrences) plus one use in the piel (2 Kgs 2:12). Excluded are the 12 niphal uses
(passive meanings where such a direct object would be impossible) and the 8 hiphil uses
(whose predominant syntagmatic patterns point to their inclusion in the "process" words
of this section).

[7] Such substantives for these verbs include only the cognate accusatives *zĕ'āqâ* (e.g.,
Esth 4:1) and *sĕ'āqâ* (e.g., Gen 27:34), such substantives as *qôl gādôl* (e.g., 2 Sam 19:5),
and *qôlî* (e.g., Ps 142:2) being better classified as adverbial accusatives (cf. *bĕqôl gādôl*,
1 Sam 28:12). The object clauses for these verbs include only direct speech — whether
attached directly (e.g., 2 Sam 19:5) or by a finite (e.g., *wayyō'mĕrû*, 2 Kgs 4:40) or non-finite
(e.g., *lē'mōr*, 2 Kgs 6:26) form of *'mr*.

[8] The predominant preposition with these verbs, and the one which governs the
nominals pertaining to this contrast, is *'el*. One other preposition, *lĕ*, has a similar function
in perhaps three instances (Hos 8:2; 1 Chr 5:20; 2 Chr 13:14). However, two other
appearances of this preposition have more particular functions (Gen 41:55 and Isa 15:15),
a characteristic of most of the other prepositions which may follow these verbs: *bĕ'ad*
(1 Sam 7:9); *bĕ* (1 Sam 28:12 and Hos 7:14); *'al* (2 Kgs 8:5, Jer 30:15; Job 31:38); *min* (Isa
65:14 and Hab 2:11); *mippĕnê* (Isa 19:20); and *neged* (Ps 88:2).

[9] Unlike $z^c q$ and $s^c q$, whose few syntagmatically variant meanings are clearly marked
by stem (see note 6 above — single exception, Judg 12:2; note textual variant), *qr'* has a host
of meanings in the qal stem which are syntagmatically similar to words of this section (e.g.,
"proclaim," "summon," "call" — see section on "process" words). With *qr'*, therefore, a
preliminary sorting out according to the three essential syntagmatic characteristics of $z^c q$
and $s^c q$ is assumed, with only those meanings which meet these criteria (e.g., "cry," "call
out," "call to" — a minority in *qr'*'s appearances as a whole) included in the paradigmatic
section in the second half of this chapter.

meaning signified by the *choice* of words following the syntagmatic patterns of z^cq and s^cq may be delineated.

Function Words — Inclusion of the Direct Object

The first essential syntagmatic pattern of z^cq and s^cq is the absence of the direct object in the majority of cases. The few times when such an object does appear demonstrate that this is a case of "object deletion" rather than of verbs which can take no direct object (see n. 7). This fact points toward those verbs' classification as "pseudo-intransitives" (Lyons, *Linquistics,* pp. 360–61). Functionally, the direct objects of z^cq and s^cq might be described as nominals with the role (or case) of "range," indicating completion or further specification of the predicate.[10]

This tendency toward object deletion is not a characteristic shared by all the words of this field. Indeed, some words, such as *'mr,* almost never occur without an object (a syntagmatic cue for the linkage of Exod 19:25 and 20:1, and a lacuna in Gen 4:8), while others do so only infrequently (e.g., *'nh, ngd*-nif, and *spr*-pi). Such words approach the status of "function" words or "copulas," grammatical "dummies" serving as the locus of tense, mood, and aspect in the sentence (Lyons, *Linquistics,* p. 346).

This difference in syntagmatic patterns indicates a basic difference in sense. While words like *'mr* necessarily point forward to completion by their objects (the actual words or speech vocalized), other words like z^cq and s^cq focus more directly on the actual activity of vocalization itself (an activity whose object, the vocalization, may often be inferred). Werner H. Schmidt, quoting G. Gerlemann on the distinction between *'mr* and *dbr*-pi, puts it this way: in the case of the verb *'mr,* "the primary concern is with the content of what is said," whereas *dbr* in the piel denotes primarily the activity of speaking (Schmidt, *"dabher," TDOT* 3, 98–99). The choice of z^cq or s^cq (or one of the words in the paradigmatic section to follow) in contrast to a "function" word (such as *'mr, 'nh, ngd*-nif, and *spr*-pi) indicates an emphasis on the *activity* of vocalization itself rather than its *content.*[11]

---

[10] R. E. Longacre, *An Anatomy of Speech Notions,* PdR Press Publications in Tagmemics, no. 3 (Lisse: Peter de Ridder Press, 1976) p. 29.

[11] Such a distinction may be helpful in describing the clauses joined to z^cq and s^cq by forms of *'mr* (e.g., *wayyō'mĕrû,* 2 Kgs 4:40; *lē'mōr,* 2 Kgs 6:26 — see n. 7). Though "functionally" such clauses may be objects of the leading verb (versus objects of the verb *'mr* or the preposition *lĕ*), semantically, the way they are attached may well indicate a shift from *activity* to *content;* i.e., "she cried out — as for the content or her cry, it was as follows . . ." Other factors, however (use of *'mr* forms with *'mr* itself, e.g., 2 Sam 3:18; outcries attached directly to z^cq or s^cq, e.g., Hab 1:2), urge one toward caution at this point.

Process Words—Non-vocal Direct Object/Presence of Indirect Object

The second and third essential syntagmatic patterns of *z'q* and *ṣ'q* concern the nature of the direct object, if present (i.e., limited to nominals associated with vocalization), and the inability of these words to take an indirect object (as opposed to an object of the preposition). Neither of these patterns is characteristic of this field as a whole. Both may be contrasted with such "process" words as *š'l, bqš, drš, pq'*-qal and hif, *ḥlh*-pi, and *ḥnn*-hitp, each of which is found in situational and literary contexts similar to those of *z'q* and *ṣ'q* (e.g., Ps 105:40; 2 Sam 12:16; Gen 25:22; Jer 36:25; 2 Kgs 13:4; Gen 42:21).

Non-vocal direct object

The function of the direct objects of *z'q* and *ṣ'q* has been described above as fitting the role (or case) of "range." For these two verbs this "complementary" function is limited solely to substantives and clauses concerned with vocalization. In contrast, the "process" words of this section may be "completed" by a wide range of objects, with the various functions of specifying the recipients, the goal, or the product of the "requesting," "petitioning," etc. (the "catch-all" category usually designated by the term "direct object"). A brief listing of such "objects" for the verbs of this section includes the following (all either in the unmarked accusative case or accompanied by the sign of the direct object, *'ēt*): (1) *things*—water (*š'l*, Judg 5:25), vessels (*š'l*, 2 Kgs 4:3), anything (*bqš*, Esth 2:15); (2) *persons*—a son (*š'l*, 2 Kgs 4:28), God (*drš*, Gen 25:22), the face of God or a person (*ḥlh*-pi, Exod 32:11; 1 Sam 13:12; Prov 19:6); and (3) *states of being or relationship*—the good (*bqš*, Ps 122:9), peace (*š'l*, Ps 122:6).

Again, this difference in syntagmatic patterns indicates a basic difference in sense. Rather than referring directly to the activity of vocalization, these verbs describe "processes" of inquiry or petition, whose object may be any of the entities listed above and within which vocalization may or may not play a central role. That this is indeed the case is supported by the frequent uses of these verbs for actions other than vocalization: *š'l*, "to borrow"; *bqš*, "to seek"; *pq'*, "to meet"; *ḥlh*-pi, "to make pleasant (the face)"; and *ḥnn*-hitp, "to make oneself favorable." It is further substantiated by those cases where the relevant "process" is explicitly carried out by some activity other than vocalization: such as entreating God (*ḥlh*-pi) by humbling oneself, 2 Chr 33:12, by turning from iniquities, Dan 9:13, or by burnt offerings, 1 Sam 13:12; or "inquiring" (*š'l*) by means of the Urim, Num 27:21. The choice of *z'q* or *ṣ'q* (or one of the words in the paradigmatic section to follow) again indicates an emphasis on the *activity* of vocalization itself, this time in contrast to a focus on the *process* of which it may or may not be a part.

Presence of indirect object

The above distinctions between the syntagmatic patterns of *z'q* and *ṣ'q* and the process words of this section focused on the nature of the "closer" or "direct" objects of these two groups of verbs. However, both groups of verbs can also take a "remoter" object than the direct objects discussed above, such as the second person suffix attached to *'el* in Hab 1:2 with *z'q* and "his servants" following *'ēt* in Gen 44:19 with *š'l.* Here the syntagmatic distinction rests upon how such a "remoter" object (designating the person "to whom" the cry is cried or the question asked) is subordinated to the verb.

In this regard, both *z'q* and *s'q* are remarkably consistent: they demonstrate a decided preference for subordination by the preposition *'el* (in 55 out of 59 cases where such a person is designated); a much less frequent use of *lĕ* (in three cases — see n. 8); and a sinqle instance where this "remoter" object is attached directly to the verb (Neh 9:28). All these cases occur most often in the absence of any substantive or clause which might be designated the "closer" or direct object (see above regarding object deletion). In contrast, the "process" word *š'l* quite frequently takes a "double" object. However, it never subordinates its "remoter" object with *'el* and seldom does so with *lĕ* (cf. 2 Kgs 8:6), but prefers to subordinate this object directly to the verb either as a verbal suffix (e.g., Gen 32:18, Judg 13:6, Ps 137:3) or a separate accusative noun (e.g., Gen 38:21 and 44:19). These general syntagmatic patterns (*z'q/s'q*'s preference for an object of the preposition and *š'l*'s preference for an object in the accusative) confirm a basic functional difference between the "remoter" objects of these two groups of verbs: the "looser" subordination with *z'q* and *s'q* is indicative of their "remoter" objects' adverbial or directional function in relation to the verb (cf. Lyons on "directional locatives," *Linguistics,* pp. 298–304); while the more direct subordination with the process words is indicative of their "remoter" objects' grammatical function as the "indirect objects" of the verb (see Lyons, *Linguistics,* pp. 295–98).

This difference in the function of their "remoter" objects points to an essential difference in the meaning of these verbs. While the "indirect object" may be said to be the "recipient" of the activity of the process words (a role Longacre labels as "the experiencer"), the object of the preposition with *z'q* and *s'q* is simply "the entity towards which a predication is directed without any necessary change of state in that entity" (a role he labels the "goal," *Speech Notions,* pp. 27–35). Thus though the process words indicate some involvement of the "addressee" in the process of which such vocalization may be a part, the "remoter" object of *z'q* and *s'q* serves solely as the goal toward which the activity of the subject is projected. The choice of *z'q* or *s'q* (or one of the words in the paradigmatic section to follow) thus indicates a relationship between the "crier" and "cried to" which is tentative and initiatory at best, in contrast to a process of petition or inquiry in which the participants are already engaged![12]

---

[12] Two alternative means of discussing the distinctions within this section would be through a comparison of the sense relations of (a) "two-place" (*z'q* and *s'q*) versus "three-place" (those uses of the "process" words); or (b) "directional" (*z'q* and *s'q*) versus "locative" (the process words) verbs (see Lyons, *Linguistics,* pp. 302–4, 350).

Action Words—Necessity of Complementary Verbs

While such words as *š'l, bqš, drš,* etc. refer to processes which may involve actions other than vocalization, other words for "kneeling," "prostration," etc. seem to refer *solely* to such non-vocal activity—whether it involves the whole person (*hwh*-hištafal; *npl*-qal and hitp; *kn'*-nif) or only various parts of the body (knees—*kr'*; hands—*prš* and *nś'; soul or heart—špk*). Not surprisingly, such words are quite easy to differentiate from *z'q* and *s'q* on the syntagmatic level, using such cues as non-vocal objects (knees, hands, etc.); lack of vocal modifiers (e.g., *bĕqôl gādôl*); and the use of niphal (e.g., *kn'*) and hithpael (e.g., *npl*) stems (which are infrequent, of variant meanings, or totally absent in the words most close syntagmatically to *z'q* and *s'q*).

The only problem with discarding this group of words from the field on the basis of such syntagmatic cues alone is the possibility that bodily activity may be used *figuratively* for the vocalization at its core, as when Hannah describes her "speaking in her heart" (*mĕdabberet 'al-libbah*) as "pouring out her soul" (*wā'ešpōk 'et napšî*—1 Sam 1:13, 15). Numerous authors have gone to great lengths to demonstrate that such actions of gesture and posture are often used in both the literature and the iconography of the ancient Near East to represent less ambiguously the relational value of vocal activity in interpersonal encounters.[13]

However, this apparent exception demonstrates a fairly reliable rule: where such actions are used figuratively for vocal activity, they are quite consistently used in conjunction with "complementary" verbs which make this vocalization explicit (e.g., the pairing of *špk lēb* and *nś' kappayim* with *rnn* in Lam 2:19). This "figurative" use thus parallels the "literal" use, with the sequential linkage of such words for bodily and vocal actions demonstrating both their *connectedness* (situationally) and their *differentiation* (semantically; e.g., *wattippōl, wattištāhû, wattō'mer*—2 Sam 14:4). Again the choice of *z'q* or *s'q* (or one of the words in the paradigmatic section to follow) indicates an emphasis on the activity of vocalization alone, not (as with both the literal and the figurative uses of these "action" words) on other actions of posture, gesture, etc. which may accompany it.[14]

---

[13] Some representative examples are Keel, *Symbolism;* Gerstenberger, *Der bittende Mensch;* and Mayer I. Gruber, *Aspects of Nonverbal Communication in the Ancient Near East,* Studa Pohl, no. 12 (Rome: Biblical Institute Press, 1980).

[14] A more difficult class of "action" words is represented by *bkh,* which seems halfway between such words for vocal lamentation as *yll*-hif and such words for physical weeping (i.e., tears) as *dm'* and *dlp.* However, several syntagmatic cues—lack of non-vocal objects (e.g., tears or water) and use of the cognate accusative (*bĕkî*) as well as vocal modifiers (*qôl gādôl*)—point toward *bkh*'s inclusion in the paradigmatic section to follow versus its classification as an "action" word.

Conclusions

Contrasting the syntagmatic patterns characteristic of these three groups of words from the field with those characteristic of $z^ʿq$ and $ṣʿq$ (and the words in the paradigmatic section to follow) enables one to posit two dimensions of meaning signified by the choice of $z^ʿq$ or $ṣʿq$ as the verb in a sentence (1) the predicate of this sentence is concerned solely with the activity of vocalization itself, not its content (versus "function" words) nor the process of which it may be a part (versus "process" words), nor any other activities which may accompany it (versus "action" words); and (2) this predicate implies no involvement of the "crier" with the "cried to" (versus "process" words), but, at best, initiates such a process through the directed "crying" of one toward another.

These syntagmatically-derived sense relations might be charted graphically as shown on page 15.

EXCURSUS: PRAYER WORDS

Given a restriction of "remoter" object (only God or gods) and, some would argue, of subject (only "men of God especially endowed with power," Stahli, "*pll* hitp., beten," *THAT* 2, 428), several of the words already studied (e.g., *šʿl, bqš, drš, ḥlh*-pi, and *ḥnn*-hitp) overlap the meanings of two words (*ʿtr*-qal and hif, and *pll*-hitp) for which such restriction is the rule (sole exception, Isa 45:14). These two words were purposefully omitted from the previous section for fear that their apparently "technical" use might have diverted attention from the general syntagmatic patterns which were its subject. However, at some point one must decide whether these obvious candidates for the field belong with the words of the syntagmatic section which has preceded them or with those of the paradigmatic section to follow.

General syntagmatic cues point in both directions. *On the one hand,* several cues place *ʿtr* and *pll* with the words to follow: (1) absence of a direct object in the majority of cases (e.g., Exod 10:18 and 1 Kgs 8:33); (2) such objects, when they occur, are limited to substantives (e.g., cognate accusative, *tĕpillâ*—2 Sam 7:27) or object clauses (e.g., Judg 13:8 and Jonah 2:2, both with *wayyōʾmer*) concerned with vocalization; and (3) they subordinate their "remoter" objects as objects of the preposition, particularly the directional preposition *ʾel* (e.g., Exod 8:26 and 1 Sam 8:6). *On the other hand,* both show affinities with the words in the final two categories of the preceding section: (1) *process words:* (a) subordination of "remoter" object by preposition *lĕ* (e.g., Exod 10:17 and Dan 9:4); (b) use of "spatial" versus "directional" prepositions (e.g., 1 Sam 1:12 with *lipnê;* cf. frequent uses with *ḥnn*-hitp); and (c) uses for actions other than vocalization (*pll*-pi "to judge," though marked by stem); and (2) *action words:* (a) with *ʿtr,* possibility of a "figurative" use, i.e., originally represented not vocal prayer but actions to appease an angry God (Albertz, "*ʿtr*, beten," *THAT* 2, 386; cf. 2 Sam 21:14 and 24:25); and (b) with *pll,* use of the hithpael stem, virtually non-existent in the words of the next section (cf. *ḥnn*).

FIELD OF HEBREW WORDS FOR VOCALIZATION
ARRANGED ACCORDING TO SYNTAGMATIC CUES

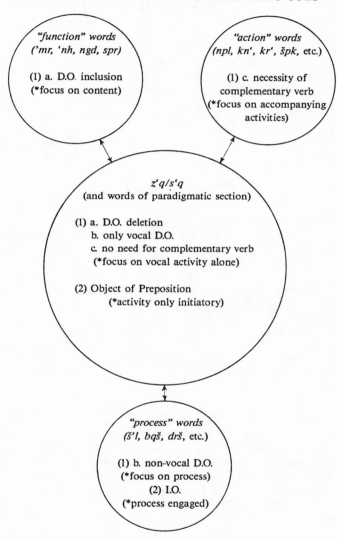

"function" words
(*'mr, 'nh, ngd, spr*)

(1) a. D.O. inclusion
(*focus on content)

"action" words
(*npl, kn', kr', špk,* etc.)

(1) c. necessity of
complementary verb
(*focus on accompanying
activities)

z'q/s'q
(and words of paradigmatic section)

(1) a. D.O. deletion
   b. only vocal D.O.
   c. no need for complementary verb
   (*focus on vocal activity alone)

(2) Object of Preposition
       (*activity only initiatory)

"process" words
(*š'l, bqš, drš,* etc.)

(1) b. non-vocal D.O.
(*focus on process)
(2) I.O.
(*process engaged)

Curiously, the seemingly "hybrid" character of *ʿtr* and *pll* syntagmatically has analogies with Jan Heller's etymological approach to the meaning of *pll*, whereby two words, *npl* and *pll*, often linked situationally (e.g., Deut 9:18, 20; Ezra 10:1) become linked semantically and formally. This creates the *combined* form, *pll*-hitp: in *etymology* closest to *npl* (hence the reflexive stem and core meaning, "bow down"), in *usage* closest to *pll* (hence the "vocal" characterstics shared with the words in the following section)![15] Though it is extremely problematic to posit theories of semantic change as grounds for syntagmatic patterns, such a theory of "mixed heritage" does seem to match the peculiar syntagmatic position of these two "technical" words for prayer in relation to the rest of the words of this field. Perhaps it also points to a "both/and" approach to these words' meaning where they possess *both* an emphasis on the *vocal activity* which they most often must include *and* an emphasis on the *process* and accompanying actions within which such vocalization most often must be set.

II. PARADIGMATIC CUES TO MEANING

If syntagmatic patterns offer cues for differentiating the meaning of *many* of the Hebrew verbs concerned with vocalization from that of $z^{ʿ}q$ and $s^{ʿ}q$, they do not offer such cues for *all* the words of their field. Indeed, as mentioned above (introduction to preceding section), *all* the words of this section conform to the three essential syntagmatic characteristics of $z^{ʿ}q$ and $s^{ʿ}q$ (with the exceptions noted in nn. 6 and 9). Therefore, this section shifts from cues for meaning in relations between words *within the sentence* to cues for meaning in relations between words *beyond the sentence*, i.e., paradigmatic cues to meaning. Here the paradigmatic relations between this group of words as a whole will serve to elucidate the meaning signified by the choice of $z^{ʿ}q$ or $s^{ʿ}q$ to fill a slot in a sentence syntagmatically amenable to them all. In this section the words will be categorized according to three essential sense relations among them: one concerned with the *function* of the vocalization, one its *content*, and one its *intensity*.

Function of the Vocalization

This group of words divides itself into five separate sets according to the function of vocalization, running from most to least inclusive.

To call (or raise the voice) — *qrʾ (nśʾ, ntn* and *rûm*-hif with *qôl*). The functional inclusiveness of this set of words may be demonstrated with *qrʾ* in several ways: (1) the variety of *direct quotes* it introduces — announcements of approaching royalty (Gen 41:43; cf. Esth 6:9, 11); battle cries (Judg 7:20); commands (Gen 45:1; cf. 2 Sam 20:16 and Jer 31:6); warnings (Lev 13:45; cf. Lam 4:15), and accusations (2 Kgs 11:14); (2) the variety of *idioms* necessary for specifying particular functions — *běšēm yhwh* (to call upon the name, "invoke,"

[15] Jan Heller, "Das Gebet im Alten Testament: Begriffsanalyse," *Communio Viatorum* 19 (1976) 159–160.

Gen 4:26); accusative with *lipnê* (to call out before one, "herald," Gen 41:43); and preposition *bĕ* (to recite from, "read," Deut 17:19);[16] and (3) the frequent use of accompanying verbs to specify meaning—followed by *šw'*, to "cry for help" (Isa 58:9 and Jonah 2:3); and by *rûm*-polal, to "extol" (Ps 66:17)![17]

To cry—z'q and s'q. Though not as wide-ranging as the first set, *z'q* and *s'q* demonstrate their relative inclusiveness as follows: (1) the variety of *direct quotes* which accompany them—cries of recognition (2 Kgs 2:12); accusatory questions (1 Sam 28:12); exclamations of despair; (1 Sam 5:10 and 2 Kgs 6:5); funeral laments (2 Sam 19:5); and prayers of lament, intercession, and penitence (Ezra 9:8; Num 12:13; Judg 10:10); (2) presence of *idioms* for specifying particular functions—with preposition *'al* (to cry against, "accuse," Job 31:38); with preposition *bĕ'ad* (to cry on behalf of, "intercede," 1 Sam 7:9); and in the imperative (summons to communal lament, Jer 25:34); and (3) the use of the directed preposition *'el*—to distinguish the two primary functions at the core of these two words' various meanings, the undirected "Schmerzensschrei" (e.g., Isa 26:17) and the directed "Hilferuf" (e.g., 2 Kgs 6:26; Albertz, *"s'q," THAT* 2:569–70). (This distinction will be dealt with more fully in the final section of this chapter.)

To groan, scream, moan, etc.—'nh-nif, *hgh, hmh, š'q,* etc![18] With this set of words, no specification of function through the use of accompanying quotations is possible, as such direct quotes are here totally lacking. This "negative" evidence might be combined with the following observations to argue that here the function of the vocalization is limited to those vocal sounds which register *pain* (the undirected "Schmerzensschrei" above): (1) absence of directional preposition *'el*—except with unusual meanings ("for," with *hmh* in Jer 48:36; cf. *lĕ*) or suggested emendations (*'al* with *'nh* in Ezek 21:12); (2) *funereal provenance*—note the clustering of these verbs with "technical" terms for mourning (e.g., *'bl*, with *'nh*, Isa 24:7) and in passages concerned with lamentation (e.g., *'nh*, four times in first chapter of Lamentations alone); and (3) explicit *opposition*—between directed (*'el*) crying *for help* from the heart (*zā'ăqû bĕlibbām*) and non-directed (no preposition) wailing *in pain* upon the bed (*yeyēlîlû 'al-miškĕbôtām,* Hos 7:14).

---

[16] This great diversity of idiomatic expressions using the verbal forms of *qr';* may explain the scarcity of nominal cognates of this verb (only *qĕrî'â;* used once, Jonah 3:2); i.e., an unadorned cognate would be so "inclusive" as to be virtually meaningless.

[17] This "tendency" with *qr'* approaches a "rule" with the other words of this set—*ns', ntn, rûm*-hif, either with or without the object *qôl.* It is indeed the variety of their complementary verbs (*rnn*—Isa 24:14 and 52:8; *s'q* —Jer 22:20; *bkh*—Gen 21:16; and *qr'*—Judg 9:7), more than any meaning of these words on their own, which places them in the same inclusive category as *qr'.*

[18] This list might go on and on (as does Albertz, *"s'q," THAT* 2, 570–71) if not for the five times or more cutoff placed on the words of this chapter (see n. 3). Here the most frequent of this set will be used to stand for the group as a whole, including such less frequent verbs as *'nq, n'q*-qal and nif, *nhq*-pi, *nhm,* and *p'h* as well as such closely related words as *yll*-hif and *bkh* (see n. 14).

To shout and yell—rnn and *rw'*. Though lack of direct quotes again renders the function of these vocalizations ambiguous, and though a minority of their appearances parallel the cries of pain of some of the words above (*rw'* with *z'q* and *bkh,* Isa 15:4; *rnn* with *ṣ'q,* Lam 2:18-19; *rw'* as cry of woman in labor, Mic 4:9, cf. *z'q* in Isa 26:17), several observations point toward the predominant function of these vocalizations as shouts of *joy, praise,* or *victory:* (1) accompaniment by *verbs and songs* of praise—verbs (*śmḥ* and *'lz* with *rnn* and *rw'*, Zeph 3:14; *gyl* with *rw'*, Zech 9:9); songs (with *rw'*, Ezra 3:11; with *rnn,* Jer 31:7); (2) *military provenance* (especially *rw'*)—infrequently a cry of defeat (Judg 7:21); more frequently a cry of victory (with *'al,* Jer 50:15); but most characteristically the "battle-cry" itself, inducing panic in the enemy (1 Sam 17:52; Isa 42:13; 2 Chr 13:15) if not serving as the instrument of destruction (Josh 6:5, 10, 16, 20); and (3) explicit *opposition* to the above "Schmerzensschrei"— (e.g., *rnn* in contrast to *ṣ'q* and *yll,* Isa 65:14).

To cry for help—šw'. Out of all the verbs of this section, this one alone approaches what might be termed a *specialized* ("speziellere," Albertz, "*ṣ'q,*" *THAT* 2:570) function. Though lacking the directional preposition *'el* in 15 out of its 24 occurrences, the particular function of this verb as a "cry for help" might be substantiated in several ways: (1) its frequent pairing with *z'q* or *ṣ'q*— Hab 1:2; Ps 88:2; Job 19:7 and 35:9; and Lam 3:8; (2) the few times an *explicit exclamation* is attached to accompanying verbs—to *z'q* (*ḥāmās,* Job 19:7); to *ṣ'q* (*ḥāmās,* Hab 1:2); to *qr'* (*hôšî'ēnî,* Ps 119:146-47); and (3) the possibility of an *etymological argument*—the restricted functions of both the nominal and verbal forms of the root *sw'* make some linkage with the root for the "saving" response, *yš',* quite tempting (cf. *BDB*'s etymological note on p. 1002).

The relations between these various sets of words categorized according to the function of the vocalization might be charted as shown in page 19.

Content of the Vocalization

This group of words divides itself into three separate sets according to the content of the vocalization, again running from most to least inclusive:

To call (or raise the voice)—qr'. The vocalizations of this set contain examples of each of the three possible categories with regard to content: (1) *extended articulations*—both attached directly (e.g., Exod 34:6) and with a form of *'mr* (e.g., Judg 9:7; 15:18; 16:28); (2) *brief* articulations (e.g., 2 Kgs 11:14); and (3) *inarticulate exclamations*—(e.g., the call of ravens, Ps 147:9). This breadth with regard to content again demonstrates the inclusiveness of this set of words for vocalization.

To cry or cry for help—z'q/ṣ'q and *šw'*. Though *z'q* and *ṣ'q* are occasionally accompanied by some rather lengthy articulations (e.g., Judg 10:10; 1 Sam 12:10; 2 Kgs 4:1), such articulations in general are much less frequent than with *qr'* (only 11 out of 128 occurrences); show a marked tendency toward brevity (2 Kgs 6:26; Hab 1:2; Job 19:7); and, if lengthier, are quite consistently set off from *z'q* or

PARADIGMATIC RELATIONS: FUNCTION OF THE VOCALIZATION

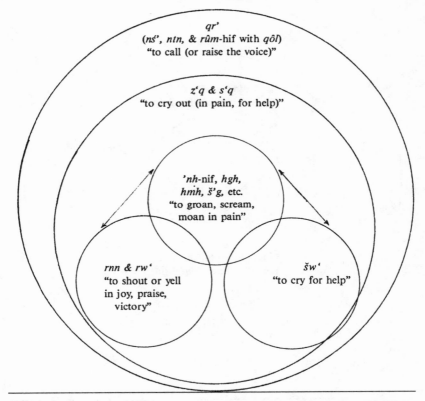

$s^ʿq$ by a form of *'mr* (see n. 11—single exception, 2 Kgs 2:12, follows a participial form in the piel). Such cues point toward brief, initial outcries which might be categorized as either: (1) *brief articulations*—note the use of *šwʿ* as a parallel verb in Hab 1:2; Ps 119:146-47; Job 19:7, and (2) *inarticulate exclamations*—of stones (Hab 2:11), land (Job 31:38); or blood (Gen 4:10; cf. Job 16:18 and Ps 9:13).

To groan or shout—'nh-nif and *rnn*. Numerous cues point toward the restriction of this set to the single category of *inarticulate exclamations* (1) lack of explicit content (see above regarding direct quotes); (2) preponderance of *non-personal* vocalizations—of the soul and heart (with *hmh*, e.g., Ps 42:6, 12; Jer 48:36); of waves (with *hmh*, e.g., Isa 51:15); of musical instruments (with *hmh*, e.g., Isa 6:11; Jer 48:36); and of animals (with *š'q*; both literally, e.g., Amos 3:4, 8; Ps 104:21; and figuratively, e.g., Ps 38:9; Jer 2:15; Job 37:4); and (3) possibility of *onomatopoeic arguments*—for cries of pain in general (*'nq, n'q, nhq, nhm, nhg, 'nh, hgh*, etc.; cf. *z'q* and *s̩'q*; see Albertz, *THAT* 2:570),

PARADIGMATIC RELATIONS: CONTENT OF THE VOCALIZATION

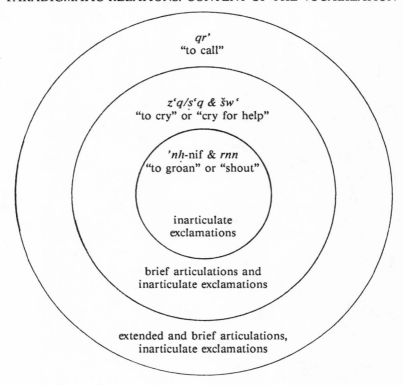

lamentation wails in particular (*yll*-hif; see *BDB,* p. 410); and the trilled shout of the battlefield (note *resh* in *rw'* and *rnn;* cf. *srh*).[19]

The above paradigmatic relations based on content might be charted as in the illustration on this page.

Intensity of the Vocalization

Though perhaps the most difficult sense relation to distinguish structurally (as opposed to situationally or literarily), intensity (in terms of volume, pitch,

---

[19] One might further divide this group between words which imply a repetitive or sustained type of exclamation (e.g., *yll?*) and those where such a temporal dimension is lacking unless indicated by form (e.g., participle of *'nh*-nif, Lam 1:21) or context (e.g., weariness provoked by continual moaning, *bĕ'anhātî,* Ps 6:7).

or emotional content) is important for the meaning of all the words of this group. It is here proposed, however, that such intensity is important in two overlapping, yet dissimilar ways:

To call or shout (*qr'* and *rnn*). Here the implied intensity is primarily one of volume, having implications with respect to range, i.e, how far the vocalization will carry over space. This is made evident by particular spatial idioms peculiar to this set of words (e.g., *bĕ'oznê* with *qr'*, Ezek 8:18). Therefore, when these words occur with adverbial modifiers intensifying the action of the verb (e.g. *bĕqôl gādôl* with *qr'*, Gen 39:14), this intensification is primarily one of volume, indicating the greater distance over which this vocalization can and should be heard (cf. Albertz, "*ṣ'q*," *THAT* 2:569).

To cry or groan or cry for help (*z'q/ṣ'q*, *'nḥ*-nif, *šw'*). Here the implied intensity primarily focuses upon the emotional dimension (of fear, of pain, of desperation, etc.), having implications for the perceived necessity under which the vocalization is uttered. This is supported by the fact that adverbial modifiers (such as *qôl gādôl*, and *bĕqôl gādôl*—see n. 7) occur primarily *not* with directed vocalizations (whose intensity, as above, might be concerned with range), but with non-directed cries of pain (where such intensification only underlines the physical or emotional "angst" out of which the vocalization arises). This observation is particularly clear with *z'q* and *ṣ'q*, where three out of the four cases in which such adverbial modifiers are used (Gen 27:34; 1 Sam 28:12; 2 Sam 19:5) not only involve non-directed cries, but arise from situations where the "already past" nature of the vocalization's impetus makes a directed "cry for help" highly unlikely.

The above paradigmatic relations based on intensity might be charted as follows:

PARADIGMATIC RELATIONS: INTENSITY OF VOCALIZATION

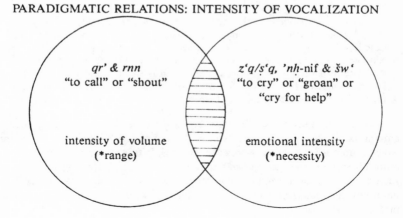

qr' & rnn
"to call" or "shout"

z'q/ṣ'q, *'nḥ*-nif & *šw'*
"to cry" or "groan" or
"cry for help"

intensity of volume
(*range)

emotional intensity
(*necessity)

Conclusions

The above paradigmatic analysis enables one to specify the meaning signified by a choice of $z'q$ or $s'q$ (versus one of their syntagmatically similar superordinates, e.g. qr'; antonym, e.g., rnn; or hyponyms, e.g., $šw'$ — see Silva, *Biblical Words,* pp. 118-35) according to the three basic dimensions of vocalization treated in this section: (1) *function* — indicates a fundamental tension between two related, but differentiated functions (a directed cry for help and an undirected cry of pain); (2) *content* — sits on the borderline between brief, articulated outcries (more characteristic of cries for help, cf. $šw'$) and a host of similar sounding inarticulate ones (more characteristic of cries of pain, cf. *'nh*-nif, etc.); and (3) *intensity* — a heightened emotional intensity is assumed, any extra stress pointing toward a function as a cry of pain.

III. CUES FOR DIFFERENTIATING AMONG THE SENSES OF $Z'Q$ AND $S'Q$

The conclusions of both the preceding sections underline a fundamental tension signified by the choice of either $z'q$ or $s'q$ as the verb of vocalization in a sentence. First, three of the four syntagmatic comparisons (direct object deletion, vocal direct object, complementary verb) focus these verbs' meaning solely on the activity of vocalization — the organizing center of their field. Then the remaining syntagmatic pattern (the object of the preposition) and two of the paradigmatic relations (content and intensity) point toward an ambiguity in the third paradigmatic relation (function) which has implications for *all* the more particular nuances this vocalization may represent (engaged/unengaged participants, articulate/inarticulate outcry, stressed/doubly stressed intensity). This ambiguity involves a tension running through the center of $z'q$'s and $s'q$'s range of meanings: the contrast between an undirected cry *of pain* and a directed cry *for help*. As Albertz states the case:

> $S'q$ differs from verbs indicating a painful reaction (*'nh*, "sigh"; *bkh*, "weep"; *yll*-hif, "howl"; et al.) in that it does not remain merely a reaction to the experienced suffering, but strives toward another dimension of meaning — one which might conceivably lead to a change in the suffering itself. . . . Thus the root $s'q$ indicates the pattern of the human cry in danger, which is simultaneously a cry of pain [Schmerzensschrei] and a cry for help [Hilferuf]. . . . Sometimes one aspect predominates, sometimes the other (Albertz, "$s'q$," *THAT* 2:569-70).

While this tension within $z'q$'s and $s'q$'s general meaning may lead to ambiguity, it also grants these words an extraordinary sensitivity to nuance which is unique vis-a-vis the words of their field. In one case, $z'q$ or $s'q$ may focus more directly on the *"pain-filled"* nature of the outcry, stressing the isolation such a "mere reaction" implies. In another, they may point toward the *"for help"* nature of the outcry, stressing the initial turning toward another such an appeal makes plain.

This distinction between related, but differing meanings is central to the ongoing argument of this dissertation. Therefore, before proceeding, three possible tests for deciding which aspect of the cry is to be emphasized in a given instance will be proposed and tested out in selected passages.

Proposed Tests

Directional prepositional phrase introduced by 'el. This is the primary syntagmatic cue derived from the preceding analysis of the syntagmatic patterns of the field. It is assumed that a "directed" cry signifies a cry *for help.*

Presence of other less functionally ambiguous words for vocalization (e.g., *'nh*-nif, cry of pain; *šw'*, cry for help). This is the primary semantic "pay-off" of the preceding analysis of the paradigmatic relations of the field.

Followed by vocabulary or narrative indicative of the "response." This test introduces an entire field of words (vocabulary of "response") and method of analysis (narrative technique) heretofore unmentioned in the analyses of this chapter. This fact, combined with the untested nature of its underlying assumption (i.e., that a cry which is responded to is most likely a cry *for help*), urges the cautious use of this particular test. Decisions based on this test alone will be tentative at best.

Selected Passages

Numbers 11:1-3

The three verbs for vocalization in this passage (*'nn*-hitpol; *ṣ'q;* and *pll*-hitp) provide the narrative framework upon which this story is built. First, these verbs contrast those who speak (people and Moses) from the one who hears and acts (God). Second, they contrast those who "complain" and "cry out" (the people) from the one who "prays" (Moses—see excursus on the restriction of object and subject for this particular verb). Third and most important, the first two verbs for vocalization contrast one type of vocal activity by the people— circumstantial (telling when God heard), undirected (*bě'oznê* designates range, not direction), and self-concerned (note hithpolel stem; cf. with "process" and "action" verbs)—with another—finite (and linked consecutively), directed (*'el-môšeh*), and intentional (leading to subsequent prayer and abatement of the crisis). All three of the proposed tests (*'el*, opposition to *'nn*, and narrative response) point toward *ṣ'q*'s function here as a cry *for help,* an initiatory turning function ideally suited to its climactic location and role in this particular narrative.

Jeremiah 48:31-33

Here the repetitive piling up of four different verbs for vocalization (*yll*-hif, *z'q, hgh, bkh*) sets the tone for the passage as a whole. Here there is no vocabulary of "response" (only repeated verbs of destruction in the perfect—*npl*, *'sp*-nif, and *šbt*-hif). Here are no directional prepositions (*'al, lě, 'el,* and *lě* all

being used to specify "for whom" the vocalizations are offered). Most important, here are three verbs (*yll*-hif, *hgh,* and *bkh*) whose function is quite
consistently a cry of pain (see section on '*nh*-nif, etc. above), confirming a similar
function for the parallel fourth term, *z'q.* The only ambiguity in this passage
arises out of the nonspecificity of such inarticulate vocalizations in general — are
they cries of pain or joy (see section on *rnn,* etc. above)? This final ambiguity
is squelched in the last verse. As gladness and joy have been taken away (v 33a),
hêdād lō' hêdād; i.e., this shouting is not the joyful shouting of those treading
grapes, but rather the shout of destruction (cf. Jer 25:30 and 51:14; Isa 16:9–10).

Psalm 22:2–6

At first glance, the use of *z'q* in v 6 of Psalm 22 seems quite straightforward,
its directional preposition ('*ēlêkā*) and vocabulary of "response" (*wĕnimlātû*)
setting this cry for help of the fathers in contrast to the non-directed groans
(*ša'ăgātî*—v 2) and calling ('*eqrā*' —v 3) of the Psalmist. However, both of the
latter terms also show indications of being cries for help—*ša'gātî* (vocative, '*ēlî;*
response, *mîšû'ātî;* articulation, *dibrê*) and '*eqrā*'; (vocative, '*ēlōhay;* response,
tā'ăneh). Thus the contrast seems to be between the explicitly directed cries for
help of the fathers which were answered (cf. *šw'* in v 25b), and the more diffuse
groans and calls of the Psalmist which are not.

However, at this point one must ask if such syntagmatic and paradigmatic
cues for meaning have now received more weight than they can or should bear.
Perhaps such variations are here only stylistic. Perhaps the form of v 6 is
influenced by earlier traditions. Perhaps, in the Psalter, all "crying out," whether
in pain or for help, functions in a petitionary fashion.

Obviously, such issues of interpretation push beyond the sentence-level
analyses of this chapter. Some context other than their word field must be
analyzed in order to discover what the biblical use of *z'q* and *s'q* might have to
offer in debates such as these. One such context, a setting in life for the directed
cry, is the topic of the following chapter.

3
A Setting in Life

Thus a literary explanation of Old Testament texts alone cannot be suffi-
cient. This also follows from the fact that the surface form of speech does
not necessarily conform with the intended meaning. Speech and literature
become somewhat clear only through the appropriate social context.
Gerstenberger, Der bittende Mensch, p. 63.

Most readers of English would not attempt to interpret the verb "cry" in the
sentence, "then we cried to the Lord," using the syntagmatic and paradigmatic
comparisons of the last chapter—unless forced to do so by a linguist. First, they
would attempt to place the sentence "situationally" by asking after the identity
of the "we"; their status over against "the Lord"; and most important, the
particular setting—either in history or day-to-day life—within which this
sentence should be understood. Quite correctly, they would recognize that even
after narrowing the range of meanings possible for this verb according to the
structure of the vocabulary, the English verb "cry" means or signifies different
things in different settings (e.g., the cry of a baby for its mother, the pedestrian
for a taxi, the accused for justice).

Again, it is the premise of this chapter that the reader of Hebrew should
attempt to interpret the verb *s'q* in the sentence *wannis'aq 'el-yhwh 'ĕlōhê
'ăbōtênû* in a similar fashion. In fact, this location of Hebrew sentences situationally is perhaps *more* essential than the foregoing location of *z'q* and *s'q*
structurally. For while the contributions of syntagmatic patterns and paradigmatic relations to the meaning of verbs associated with vocalization may be quite
similar for biblical Hebrew and modern English (due to basic syntactical structures shared by most languages; e.g., transitivity, opposition, etc.), the contributions of various social settings may not (due to the differing social structures
within which such vocalizations would be uttered). In other words, even if the
English "cry" is an accurate translation of the general semantic possibilities of
the Hebrew *s'q,* a "cry" may not mean or signify the same thing within a given
setting in the life of ancient Israel as it would in a similar setting today (cf. Hans
Walter Wolff's identification of *z'q* in the imperative as a summons to a "national
festival of lamentation)![1]

[1] Hans Walter Wolff, "Der Aufruf zur Volksklage," *Zeitschrift für die alttestamentliche
Wissenschaft* 76 (1964) 55.

It would be tempting to begin here with those recurring historical summaries mentioned in the introduction to this dissertation which recount a "cry" foundational for the Old Testament story as a whole (e.g., Num 20:16; Deut 26:7; Josh 24:7; cf. 1 Sam 12:8 and Neh 9:9). However, not only is the historical referent of these passages difficult to place precisely (i.e., cry in bondage, Deut 26:7; or cry at the sea, Josh 24:7?), their social setting in the life of Israel has proven an ongoing vexation (i.e., von Rad's "credos" versus Weiser, Fohrer, Rast, Brekelmans, Hyatt, etc.).[2]

There is, however, another social setting for the use of z^cq and s^cq within the Old Testament scriptures which is much more straightforward situationally—the cry of the legally marginal to the king. This "cry" plays an integral role in five Old Testament narratives (2 Sam 14:1-24; 2 Kgs 6:24-31; 1 Kgs 20:35-43; 2 Kgs 8:1-6; and 2 Sam 19:25-31).[3] The consistency of this narrative use allows this setting in the life of Israel to be described quite precisely with regard to: (a) the situation of need (necessity of a legal hearing); (b) the identity of the participants (a person who is legally marginal and the king); and (c) the actual characteristics of the request (a five-fold form described below).[4] Furthermore, in four of the five narratives, the particular form of the "cry" is remarkably consistent (a directed, verbal form of z^cq or s^cq—2 Kgs 6:26; 1 Kgs 20:39; 2 Kgs 8:5; and 2 Sam 19:29) pointing toward this "cry's" function as a subset of the last chapter's cry *for help*.

In the first half of this chapter, this setting in life for the directed cry will be described in detail according to the three primary situational categories listed above. In the second half, three similar situational settings (the cry of the oppressed, the cry of the raped, and the cry of the blood) will be compared with this setting of the marginal's cry to the king in order to test the possibility of

---

[2] For a more complete bibliography see Patrick D. Miller, Jr., *The Divine Warrior in Early Israel*, Harvard Semitic Monographs, vol. 5 (Cambridge Harvard University Press, 1973) p. 167.

[3] The "concrete pictures" provided by such narrative material are here given priority over the highly figurative and stereotyped language of biblical poetry for providing the detailed social categories (of situation, participants, and form of interaction) necessary for the arguments of this chapter. Compare Patrick D. Miller's similar attempt to render the language of the Psalms more concrete by relating the "predicaments" of the laments to "narrative and historical contexts" outside the Psalter. See Patrick D. Miller, Jr., "Trouble and Woe: Interpreting the Biblical Laments," *Interpretation* 37 (Jan 1983) 36.

[4] The categories listed here are adaptations of Erhard S. Gerstenberger's five constitutive elements of an interpersonal "Bittsituation" ("Mangel, Besitzverteilung, Rangordnung, Solidaritat und die aktuellen Ausdrucksmerkmale der Bitte," Gerstenberger, *Der bittende Mensch*, p. 19) organized under three major headings. The assumption is that the cry of the marginal to the king represents a particular case of Gerstenberger's "Bittsituation" within which these general elements of the inter-human petition take on a quite specific and consistent shape.

semantic carry-over from one precisely defined social setting to others which are more or less analogous.

I. THE CRY OF THE LEGALLY MARGINAL TO THE KING

Situation of Need—Necessity of a Legal Hearing

A prerequisite for any cry "for help" from one person to another is a situation of need. In all five narratives, the necessity which provokes the type of emotionally intense outcry signified by a choice of $z'q$ or $s'q$ is quite precise—the need for someone of judicial authority to decide another person's case. Sometimes this need for a decision arises out of a decision previously rendered against a person who then appeals for a counter-decision from another (2 Sam 14:5-7). Other times, the needed decision is an initial one, required either to overturn traditional procedures (of land forfeiture, 2 Kgs 8:1-3) or previous agreements (regarding prisoners of war, 1 Kgs 20:39-40); or because the case itself is so difficult or extreme (2 Kgs 6:28-29; cf. 1 Kgs 3:16-28). The loss of the right to satisfy this basic need for legal decision can be used elsewhere to accentuate the utter destitution of the person petitioning another (2 Sam 19:29), highlighting the fact that this person's fate is no longer in his or her own hands, but solely those of another ("do whatever pleases you," 2 Sam 19:28).

That this need for a legal hearing was no "casual" necessity in the social world of ancient Israel[5] is made obvious by the deprivations which threaten if the need for judicial decision goes unmet or leads to an unfavorable verdict: lack of food, specifically a neighbor's cannibalized son (2 Kgs 6:28-29); lack of life, due to an apparent breaking of a "life-threatening" contract (1 Kgs 20:39); and

---

[5] This is apparently the assumption of Hans Jochen Boecker, who designates the use of $s'q$ in 2 Kgs 8:1-6 "technical" in opposition to other uses arising from situations he labels "acute" or "life and death." See Hans Jochen Boecker, *Redeformen des Rechtslebens im Alten Testament,* Wissenschaftliche Monographien zum Alten und Neuen Testament, Bd. 14 (Neukirchen-Vluyn: Neukirchener Verlag, 1964) pp. 62–63. Similar is the stance of Gerhard von Rad, *Genesis: A Commentary,* 2d ed., trans. by John H. Marks, The Old Testament Library (Philadelphia: Westminster Press, 1972) pp. 106 and 211 (cf. Gerhard von Rad, *Old Testament Theology,* trans. by D. M. G. Stalker [New York: Harper & Row, 1962] p. 157 n. 34, and p. 415 n. 65) and Hasel, "$z\bar{a}'aq$," *TDOT* 4:118-19. One wonders if such writers are so concerned with either the substantiation or rejection of parallels between the legal use of $z'q$ and $s'q$ in the Old Testament and certain aspects of medieval German judicial procedure (namely the "Zetergeschrei") that they have either under-stressed or overstressed the *continuity* between this particular type of "Hilferuf" and the myriad other uses of these words in the scriptures. Though at other points this dissertation will emphasize the *discontinuity* between this legal cry for help and other types of cries in the Old Testament (especially the undirected cry of pain), at this point a basic *continuity* is grounded in one fundamental dimension of the many situations out of which this general cry arises—the characteristically "necessary" nature of the crier's need (cf. the aspect of "emotional intensity" which is assumed with the choice of either $z'q$ or $s'q$, chap. 2).

lack of house and land, a woman's primary hope for sustenance following the assumed death of her husband (2 Kgs 8:5). 2 Sam 14:7 makes explicit the culturally determined connection between what might to us seem a more "everyday" deprivation (lack of a male child) and what was to the people of the Old Testament truly "life-threatening" by citing what would be the result of her clan's decision being allowed to stand: "Thus they would quench my coal which is left and leave to my husband neither name nor remnant upon the face of the earth." This is strong language in the social world of the Old Testament, stretching beyond a threat to the life of a single individual to include the future of an entire family (cf. *šēm* with respect to families — Deut 25:6; Ruth 4:10; 2 Sam 18:18; and nation — Deut 7:24; 9:14; Nah 1:14; also *šēm ûšĕ'ār* — Isa 14:22).

The situation in which the cry "for help" arises is thus one of life or death. It, therefore, is to be distinguished from other narrative outcries in the Old Testament (in the midst of regional famine, Gen 41:55; sudden illness, 2 Kgs 4:40; or personal combat, 1 Kgs 22:32) *not* in terms of a diminution of the threat involved, but by the specific way in which this particular threat is to be countered, i.e, through legal appeal.

The Identity of the Participants — Marginal/King

This section will be divided into three sub-sections dealing with different aspects of the *relationship* between the "crier" and the "cried to" essential to understanding the specific meaning of the cry directed from one to another.

Uneven distribution of goods — inequality of judicial power.

At the heart of any cry for help from one person to another is a recognition of an inequality of goods between the "crier" and the "cried to." In all five of the narratives of this section, the particular inequality between the persons involved is one of judicial power; i.e., the power to render judicial decisions which will be recognized by others. While this uneven distribution of legal power is the driving force behind all appeals for hearing directed toward the courts of a given society (e.g., the request of Boaz for his fellow Elders to "turn aside" and "sit" in the court of the gate, Ruth 4:1-6), in certain situations this inequality — and thus the requests arising therefrom — approach the extreme.

The king

At one end of Israel's spectrum of legal power stood the king. Though preceded by a long line of individuals who were recognized as possessing an "excess" in the realm of judicial authority (from Moses, Exod 18:13-26; to Joshua, Josh 7:16-26; the lesser "judges," Judg 10:1-5 and 12:8-15; and Samuel and sons, 1 Sam 7:16-17, 12:3-5, cf. 1 Sam 8:1-3), the coming of the monarchy to Israel represented something new in the judicial structures of Israel's life as a nation.[6] Judicial authority was not just *one* of *many* characteristics possessed by the king of Israel, but was foundational for the establishment of the monarchy in general (cf. the request of the tribes for a king "to judge us," *lĕšoptēnû*, 1 Sam 8:5) and a motivating force behind the desire for the throne in particular (e.g., 2 Sam 15:4). Therefore, its proper execution was continually held up as representative of the highest kingly ideals (David — 2 Sam 12:1-6, cf. 8:15; Absalom — 2 Sam 15:2-6; and Solomon — 1 Kgs 3:16-28, cf. 7:7). Perhaps in this respect more than many others, Israel's monarchy was closest to those of "all the nations" (*kĕkol-haggôyim*, 1 Sam 8:5).[7] For despite Israel's ongoing distrust of kingship in general (as in one layer of the DtrH) and attempts to bring the king under the law (Deut 17:18-20), in the realm of judicial decision, the king's wisdom might approach that of God himself (1 Kgs 3:28), his power over life and death that of God's angels ("my lord the king is like the angel of God," 2 Sam 19:28; cf. 2 Sam 14:17, 20). Indeed, when one approached the king in hopes of legal hearing, one's gestures, posture, and manner of appeal mimic those used by the supplicant in his or her approach to God (see below, "the approach of the marginal").[8] This exalted status of the king in the legal setting explains why the king of Israel feels compelled to counter the Samaritan woman's "Help, my lord, O King!" (*hôšî'â 'ădōnî hammelek*, 2 Kgs 6:26), with a reminder of the distinction between the earthly and the heavenly king's power, "If the Lord will not help you (*yôšî'ēk*), whence shall I help you (*'ôšî'ēk*), from the threshing floor, or the wine press (2 Kgs 6:27)?" If the woman expects the king to provide food in

---

[6] The relationship between this new "court of the king" and the other judicial bodies recognized by Israel was undoubtedly complex. For example, see the three-fold system of (a) communal jurisdictions of elders; (b) jurisdiction of the king — in person and through appointed judges; and (c) jurisdiction of priests — especially with regard to cultic laws; in Roland de Vaux, *Ancient Israel,* 2 vols. (New York: McGraw-Hill Book Co., 1961) 1:152. Some have suggested that even these complex relationships varied according to time and circumstance, such as any circumstance which might be labeled "military." See Georg Christian Macholz, "Die Stellung des Königs in der israelitischen Gerichtsverfassung, *Zeitschrift für die alttestamentliche Wissenschafte* 84 (1972) pp. 17-82. In fact, the Israelite judicial system probably always retained a degree of "informality" and "irregularity" unacceptable within larger and more homogeneous societies. See the characterization of the Israelite legal system in Johannes Pederson, *Israel: Its Life and Culture,* 4 vols. in 2 (London: Oxford University Press, 1926) 1:409-10. Compare the rejection of German parallels in Albertz, "*s'q,*" *THAT* 2: 572 and Hasel, "*zā'aq,*" *TDOT* 4:118.

[7] See Roland de Vaux's citations of the preambles of Mesopotamian codes, the poems of Ras Shamra, and Aramaen and Phoenician inscriptions in support of the thesis that the virtue of justice was the first quality of a king in the ancient Near East in de Vaux, *Ancient Israel,* 1:151.

[8] Using the iconography of Babylonia and Egypt, Othmar Keel demonstrates a striking correlation between the gestures and posture with which individuals approached the king for judicial hearing and those with which they would approach their god(s) in prayer. For example, compare figures 390 and 393 with 412, 414, 415, and 426 in Keel, *Symbolism,* pp. 288-89, 309-11, 317.

famine, she is sadly mistaken — such power is God's alone. However, if she cries out for judicial hearing, the king can and does respond — for in this judicial realm, the king's saving power approaches that of God.

The widow

At the other end of Israel's spectrum of legal power stood the widow (*'almānâ*). Though women in the ancient Near East are occasionally portrayed exercising the economic and legal rights which were a matter of course for the male property holders of their society, such did not appear to be the case in Israel.[9] In the legal codes of the Old Testament, a woman existed as a "legal nonperson," mentioned only in those particular cases where a responsible male was lacking, a woman required special protection, or sexual offenses or roles were at issue![10] What few legal rights an Israelite woman possessed, she exercised only in conjunction with a male "head of the household," either father, husband, or son (cf. Deut 21:19, 22:15, etc.). It is the male-derived and male-dependent nature of a woman's legal power within the social structures of ancient Israel which made the status of the widowed or divorced woman so "existentially prec~rious" (Bird, "Images of Women," p. 265) and which linked them in the legal codes with those other legal "marginals" — the orphan (*yātôm*) and the resident alien (*gēr* — Deut 24:17-18 and 27:19; Jer 7:6 and 22:3; Zech 7:10; see below, "the cry of the oppressed"). The "second-hand" status of the woman in the legal setting explains the Shunammite woman's response to Elisha's offer to speak on her behalf to the king or the commander of the army: "I dwell among my own people" (*bětôk 'ammî 'ānōkî yōšābet*, 2 Kgs 4:13). This family "connectedness" is the very thing which the legally marginal person — widow, orphan, resident alien — lacked, and the key social characteristic which placed them at the absolute bottom of the legal hierarchy.

The widow and the king

The precarious situation of a widow in need of judicial decision is now painfully obvious. Lacking any right to testify in the ordinary Israelite judicial

---

[9] See Carol L. Meyer, "The Roots of Restriction: Women in Early Israel," in *The Bible and Liberation: Political and Social Hermeneutics,* ed. by Norman K. Gottwald (Maryknoll: Orbis Books, 1983) p. 293. One might here cite the late Sumerian reports describing the unconcerned and unafraid attitude of women appearing in court; records from Nippur indicating the judicial role of women in divorce courts; and documents from Nuzi demonstrating a female slave's ability to conclude legal transactions and serve as a partner to a lawsuit. All three are listed in Ilse Seibert, *Women in Ancient Near East,* trans. by Marianne Herzfeld (Leipzig: Edition Leipzig, 1974) pp. 13, 17-18, 22. Such data stands in sharp contrast to Josephus' observation that in Israel women were not even permitted to give evidence in court (de Vaux, *Ancient Israel,* 1:156).

[10] Phyllis A. Bird, "Images of Women in the Old Testament," in *The Bible and Liberation: Political and Social Hermeneutics,* ed. by Norman K. Gottwald (Maryknoll: Orbis Books, 1983) p. 264.

proceedings (Boecker, *Redeformen,* p. 63), she might pray that Israel would live up to the "ideal" preserved in its "special protection" clauses (again, see "cry of the oppressed" below), or that an "intercessor" such as Boaz (Ruth 4:1–6) or Elisha (2 Kgs 4:11–17) would come her way. But, in practice, this widow's only hope might be to throw herself at the feet of the only one whose legal "excess" of power far outweighed her legal "deficit" of the same—that is, the king. In this marginal's cry for help to the king rested, perhaps, her only chance of "salvation," given the social structures within which she lived, or died.

An ordering of rank — acceptance of designated roles.

Given th: extreme inequality of goods between the marginal and the king, an intense cry directed from the former to the latter could easily be misunderstood as the cry of an angry accuser (crying against the king for his failure to protect his subjects) or the cry of a desperate attacker (crying out in hopes of startling her or his target). In order for such a cry to function as a cry "for help," its "crier" must accept the social role designated for her or him over against the person she or he cries out to.

That such an acceptance of designated roles is operant in the five narratives of this section is made strikingly evident by the use of disguises in two of them. While two of the narratives involve those archetypical legal marginals, the widow (or more precisely, widows by implication, i.e., acting in a legal situation independently of a male head of household; 2 Kgs 6:24–31 and 2 Kgs 8:1–6) and a third uses the process of appeal to the king only to underline the destitute nature of this person's position (i.e., he has forfeited even the appeal process open to society's legally marginal, 2 Sam 19:25–31), the two remaining cases involve two decidedly non-marginal types: Joab the military commander (2 Sam 14:1–24) and an unnamed prophet (1 Kgs 20:35–43). In these two cases, "revolutionary" processes are afoot—the "changing of the course of affairs" regarding the exile of Absalom (2 Sam 14:20) and the condemnation of Ahab's leniency regarding the "ban" (1 Kgs 20:42). How further such "processes" without incurring the fatal consequences such "treasonous" activity would surely entail? By taking on the designated role of the legally marginal in an appeal to the king, an approach whose every posture, gesture, and vocalization underlines its decidedly "non-revolutionary" character.

In 2 Sam 14:2, the disguise for Joab's accomplice is described in detail: "Pretend to be a mourner, and put on mourning garments; do not anoint yourself with oil, but behave like a woman who has been mourning many days for the dead," i.e., like a widow (v 5), who has lost her husband, one son, and is threatened with the loss of the other. In 1 Kgs 20:38, the adopted role and subsequent disguise are not so clear-cut: "disguising himself with a bandage over his eyes." Most likely, this particular "cover" is dictated by the message to be conveyed, i.e., a case involving the taking of prisoners of war. Here the most likely "marginal" role is not the widow, orphan, or resident alien, but that of one of the few adult male Israelites whom the legal codes group with such—the blind man (Deut 27:18, 19; cf. Job 29:13, 15).

And so by the use of disguises, Joab and the prophet lure the king into adopting his traditional role vis-a-vis the legally marginal—only to reveal their true intentions when the king has condemned himself (1 Kgs 20:41) or seen through the subterfuge (2 Sam 14:19, cf. Nathan's identical ploy in which he uses a fictitious, third-party case to condemn the king, 2 Sam 12:1-15). That the king could be so easily duped into playing the role of judge in relation to such seemingly transparent "marginals" betrays both the prevalence *of* and fixity of roles *within* this particular process of legal decision. The king, approached by a widow (or other person whose marginality is evident in legal terms, e.g., the blind man above) and addressed with a "cry," hears that "cry" not as a "cry of accusation" or "attack," but a "cry for help." Why? Because this cry of the marginal to the king for legal hearing is both familiar and fundamental to the social structures within which both the king and the marginal move and speak and act.

An appeal to solidarity—the king as protector of the marginal.

Unless the widows or other legally marginal persons are acting in conjunction with someone more powerful than themselves (as is the case in 2 Sam 14:1-24), a "revolutionary" stance would be worse than foolish on their part. Such persons, acting alone, are virtually powerless beside the king. But persons who cry for help do so *not* on the basis of any power they possess. Indeed, their cries signify the very powerlessness which lays claim on another's response. The paradox within the social world of the ancient Near East is that the greater this gap in relative power, the greater the responsibility of the powerful to respond— especially if the *powerful* person is a *king* and the *powerless* person one who is *legally marginal,* e.g., widow, orphan, or resident alien.

Continually in the inscriptions of the ancient Near East, the solidarity of the king with the legally precarious existence of the marginals is seen as the key test for the success or failure of particular dynasties. On the one hand, Hammurabi declares the success of his reign:

> In my bosom I carried the peoples of the land of Sumer and Akkad;
>> they prospered under my protection;
> I always governed them in peace;
>> I sheltered them in my wisdom.
> In order that the strong might not oppress the weak
>> *that justice might be dealt the orphan and the widow* . . .[11]

On the other hand, in the legend of King Keret, the following accusation is leveled against the king:

---

[11] James B. Pritchard, ed., *Ancient Near Eastern Texts Relating to the Old Testament,* 3d ed. with Supplement (Princeton: Princeton University Press, 1972) p. 178. Hereafter cited as *ANET.* Italics in the quotations on this and the following page are my own.

Thou hast let thy hand fall into mischief.
Thou judgest not the cause of the widow
   Nor adjudicatist the case of the wretched. (*ANET,* p. 149)

So fundamental is this test of legal protection of the marginal that it became the decisive characteristic of any person who would claim the legitimate exercise of power, such as Daniel in the Tale of Aqhat:

Straightway Daniel the Rapha-man
   Forthwith Ghazir the Harnam [iyy]-man
Is upright, sitting before the gate
   Beneath a mighty tree on the threshing floor
Judging the cause of the widow
   Adjudicating the case of the fatherless (*ANET,* p. 151)

In this respect, the social world of ancient Israel, and the relationship of the legally marginal and the king within it, were little different. The assumed role of the king as legal defender of the marginal undergirds the specific content of both prophetic commands and accusations:

and do no wrong or violence to the *alien,*
   the *fatherless,* and the *widow* (Jer 22:3).
your princes are rebels and companions of thieves
   everyone loves a bribe and runs after gifts,
they do not defend the *fatherless*
   and the *widow's* cause does not come to them (Isa 1:23).

Furthermore, as is often the case with similar texts in the ancient Near East, the king's responsibility is often expanded to include others whose precariousness before the law is not as easily explicable as the widow, orphan, and resident alien's lack of a male head of household (see section on the "cry of the oppressed" below):

for he [the king] delivers *the needy* when he calls,
   the *poor* and *him who has no helper* (Ps 72:12).
If a king judges the *poor* with equity,
   his throne will be established for ever (Prov 29:14).
He [Josiah] judged the cause of the *poor* and the *needy;*
   then it was well (Jer 22:16).

The specific identities and detailed disguises of the "criers" in the narratives of this section thus become doubly significant. Not only would the identity of a widow serve a "preventive" role in an encounter with the king (precluding her cry from being heard as a cry of attack, etc.); it would also serve a strongly "facilitative" one (due to the king's special responsibility to protect those who were marginal in a legal sense). The cry of the legally marginal to the king, though perhaps an appeal of *last resort,* was not a cry *without hope,* due to the particular shape of the social system within which it was uttered.

Actual Characteristics of the Request—A Five-fold Form

If the cry of the marginal to the king is part of a process of legal appeal within which the roles of "crier" and "cried to" are fixed by the society in which it takes place and accepted by the particular participants it involves, then one would expect the actual *form* of interaction (including cues of gesture and posture as well as speech)[12] to assume a similar fixity and acceptance in the literature which records such. It is here argued that the five narratives of this section *together* do just that, according to a five-fold form which might be described as follows (see chart on pages 36 and 37).

The king—"in passing"

The picture of the king seated on his throne was a symbol of the king as *judge* throughout the cultures of the ancient Near East (see Keel, *Symbolism,* fig. 283–86, p. 390). In this, Israel was no different. Whether the seat of judgment was located in the gates of the city (2 Sam 19:9) or the Hall of Judgment (1 Kgs 7:7), its occupation (*yšb*) by the king was an indication that the court of the king was now "in session" (2 Sam 19:9, cf. Exod 18:14 and Isa 16:5; note how Absalom, aspirant to the throne, may only stand beside the way, 2 Sam 15:2).

Given this fact, it is noteworthy that while two of the narratives of this section make such a setting possible (2 Sam 14:1–24 and 2 Kgs 8:1–6), neither makes it explicit. More important, in the latter case, the encounter between the widow and the king takes place while the king is otherwise involved (note the dependent clause introduced by *wayĕhî* followed by the main clause with *wĕhinneh,* v 5). Rather than the king "sitting" in judgment, he is diverted from other business to hear the case of the widow.

This element of interruption is combined with a noncourt setting in the remaining three narratives (2 Kgs 6:24–31; 1 Kgs 20:35–43; 2 Sam 19:25–31, cf. v 19). Furthermore, for the first two, the form is identical: *wayĕhî* plus participle *'ōbēr* plus disjunctive *waw* (2 Kgs 6:26 and 1 Kgs 20:39). *While* the king is passing by on other business, he is *interrupted* by the cry of a marginal. This *in medias res* nature of the marginal's hearing underlines the precarious nature of these people's legal rights even vis-a-vis the king, their supposed protector. Divorced from the order imposed by a formal court (with the procedures, functionaries, and furnishings such would provide), the posture, gesture, and speech of the suppliant become all the more important. For here, these alone will determine whether a case will be heard—or the king will simply continue "passing by."

---

[12] Gerstenberger goes so far as to grant preference for "actions" over "speech" (as in content) as cues to underlying settings in life due to his belief in the fixity of such actions, gestures, posture, etc. in situations of inter-human petitions (Gerstenberger, *Der bittende Mensch,* p. 63).

The marginal — the approach

Given the importance of posture, gesture, etc. on the part of the marginal, it is surprising how scant are their remnants in the texts of this section. Besides the importance of appearance (to signal identity — as underlined by the discussion of disguises above), the approach of the marginal might be summarized according to three elements, only the last of which is constant:

(1) *The drawing near.* As one would expect, when the king was seated in court, those who wanted a hearing would necessarily "come" (*bô'*) before him (e.g., 2 Sam 12:1, 15:4, 19:9, etc.). Again, notably, this "drawing near" occurs explicitly in only one of the narratives of this section (2 Sam 14:4)![13] Two of the narratives describe this movement on the part of the petitioner with less characteristic verbs (*yrd*, 2 Sam 19:25; *yṣ'*, 2 Kgs 8:3), again pointing toward the out-of-court locus for these proceedings. The remaining two cases (2 Kgs 6:24-31 and 1 Kgs 20:35-43) omit this "drawing near" entirely. The reason is obvious: in this more haphazard legal setting, it is the king, engaged in other business, who inadvertently "draws near" (see participle *'ōbēr* in section above).

(2) *Posture and gestures.* In a formal proceeding, the suppliants drew near to the seated king and "stood," *'md* (1 Kgs 3:16; cf. Keel, *Symbolism,* figs. 283-86, 390, pp. 206-7, 288). Such references are totally lacking in these narratives. Indeed, the only narrative which makes any reference to gesture and posture (2 Sam 14:1-24) states just the opposite, i.e., the disguised widow fell on her face (*npl*) and prostrated herself (*šḥh*-hithpalel, 2 Sam 14:4). Whether or not such posture is more characteristic of legal procedure in non-court settings (cf. 2 Sam 19:19, Keel, *Symbolism,* figs. 429 and 430, p. 320), the absence of any other such references in these narratives is striking — if only for the inordinate emphasis it places on the one consistent element of the approach which remains.

(3) *The cry.* In the absence of other cues regarding the approach of the marginal, the narrative weight assumed by this vocalization should now be apparent. In four of the five narratives (exception 2 Sam 14:1-24 — see above), this outcry is the first and only signal regarding the manner in which the marginal approaches and the process she or he seeks to initiate. The significance of word choice at this particular point cannot, therefore, be overemphasized.

As stated in the introduction to this chapter, and with reference to the same four out of five narratives cited above (2 Kgs. 6:24-31; 1 Kgs 20:35-43; 2 Kgs 8:1-6; and 2 Sam 19:25-31), the word chosen for this vocalization is one or the other of the word-pair *z'q/ṣ'q* — indicating brief, intense, initiatory vocal activity. In all four cases, this "cry" is further defined by an accompanying prepositional phrase (three times, *'el-hammelek;* one time, *'ēlāyw*) — indicating this is not an undirected cry "of pain" but a directed cry "for help." In one case this "cry" occurs with no direct object (2 Sam 19:29); in one with a prepositional

---

[13] Note how the absence of an object for the leading verb supports the proposed *wattābō'* behind the *LXX* as opposed to the *wattō'mer* of the MT. See chap. 2 on "function" words.

THE ACTUAL CHARACTERISTICS

	2 Sam 14:1-24	2 Kgs 6:24-31
(1) The King — "In Passing"		"now as the king was passing by," v 26
		wayĕhî + *'ōbēr* + disjunctive waw
(2) The Marginal — The Approach		
-drawing near	-*bô'*, v4 (textual note)	-king draws near
-posture/gestures	-*npl* and *šhh*, v 4	-none
-the cry	*ʾmr* and *hôši'â*, v 4	-*sā'ăgâ*, *'ēlāyw*, *lē'mōr*, *hôšî'â*, v 26
(3) The King's Reply	"What is your trouble?"	"What is your (trouble)?"
mah-lāk	*mah-lāk*, v 5	*mah-lāk*, v 28
(4) The Marginal — Statement of the Case	"She answered, 'I am a widow' "	"She answered, 'This woman said to me . . .' "
	wattō'mer vv 5b–7, 12a, 13–17, etc.	*wattō'mer* vv 28b–29
(5) The King — Judgment	"go," *lĕkî*, v 8; "bring," *wahăbē'tô*, v 10; etc.	("thus may God do to me," *ya'ăśeh*, v 31)

OF THE REQUEST

1 Kgs 20:35–43	*2 Kgs 8:1–6*	*2 Sam 19:25–31*
"now as the king was passing by," v 39	"now as he was telling the king," v 5	(cf. v 19, "as he was about to cross the Jordan")
wayĕhî + *ʿōbēr* + disjunctive waw	*wayĕhî* + *wĕhinnēh*	*bĕʿobrô*
-king draws near	-*yṣ'*, v 3	-*yrd*, v 25
-none	-none	-none (cf. v 19)
ṣāʿaq, 'el-hammelek, wayyōʾmer, (4), v 39	-*sōʿeqet, 'el-hammelek*, v 5 (cf. v 3)	-*wĕliẓʿōq, 'el-hammalek*, v 29
	"When the king asked the woman . . ."	
	wayyišʾal, v 6	
"and said, 'Your servant went out . . .' "	"she told him"	("he answered 'My Lord, the king . . .' "
wayyōʾmer, vv 39b–40a	*wattĕsapper*, v 6	*wayyōʾmar*, vv 27–29)
("thus [is] your judgment," v 40; "then the king went," *wayyēlek*, v 43)	"restore," *hāšēb*, v 6	"you shall divide the land," *taḥlēqû*, v 30

phrase designating the reference of the appeal (*'al-bêtah wĕ'al-śādah,* 2 Kgs. 8:5; cf. *'el-bêtah wĕ'el-śādah,* 2 Kgs 8:3). In one case the object of the verb is a full explication of the case, introduced by *wayyō'mer* (1 Kgs. 20:39); in the remaining case, the content of the cry itself, introduced by *lē'mōr* (2 Kgs 6:26). This final case is significant because the specific content of this brief, articulate outcry (*hôśî'â 'ădōnî hammelek*) holds out the potential of linkage not only with other "dissimilar" cries with legal overtones (e.g., *hāmās* in Hab 1:2 and Job 19:7), but with the remarkably similar cry of the remaining narrative (*hôśî'â hammelek* introduced by *'mr,* 2 Sam 14:4), making the possibility that this represents a variant cry and an alternative legal process extremely unlikely.

Though a summary statement regarding the significance of this word choice for these narratives must be postponed until the "Conclusions" at the end of this section, its *consistency within* and *centrality for* this "form" should here be stressed again. It is *this cry alone* which interrupts the "passing by" of the king and initiates a request for hearing by the marginal. On the efficacy of this cry rests the course of all that follows, matters of life and death for the marginal.

The king's reply (mah-lāk)

Up to this point, the formal setting of the hearing of cases in the gates or king's court has been contrasted with the more precarious procedure of the marginal's cry to the king in passing. At least one of the narratives of this section (1 Kgs 20:35–43) here reverts to a form indistinguishable from such a formal procedure, immediately moving to the statement of the case by the marginal and the ensuing judgment by the king (the two sections of the form to follow). A second narrative employs the cry only as a rhetorical device within the suppliant's description of his situation (2 Sam 19:25–31) and is thus irrelevant for this stage of the procedure. A third narrative (2 Kgs 8:1–6) follows the cry with an unspecified inquiry by the king (*š'l*) and a response by the woman (*spr*-pi, v 6). The remaining two narratives elucidate just what the content and function of this "inquiry" might be (2 Sam 14:1–24 and 2 Kgs 6:24–31).

The king at this stage has heard an intense cry for help, recognized its crier as a marginal, and, in one case (2 Kgs 6:27), clarified the limits of "saving" power within his grasp. He now turns to the "crier" and directs to her or him a brief question, "What is your (trouble)?" (*mah-lāk,* 2 Sam 14:5 and 2 Kgs 6:28). Though on the surface this inquiry appears to be quite open-ended (cf. the settings of 1 Kgs 1:16, 2 Kgs 3:13, and Gen 21:17), *within this context* of strictly defined participants and situations of need, its function is quite precise—it indicates the marginal's cry has been heard, correctly interpreted (as a cry for legal hearing), and accepted. The process is now engaged. The king stops his other activities and turns to hear the case.

The marginal—statement of the case

Given the cue to proceed, the marginal now states her or his case. From here on out, the narratives of this section differ little from other narratives which describe a legal procedure before the king (cf. 1 Kgs 3:16-25). While one of these narratives incorporates the cry in this part of the procedure (2 Sam 19:24-30) and another refers to this statement of the case only obliquely (*spr*-pi, 2 Kgs 8:6), for the remaining three cases, the bulk of the narrative is taken up by this section of the outline.

Though it would be interesting to list various common elements within this section of the form (e.g., use of interjections — *hinnēh,* 1 Kgs 20:39 and 2 Sam 14:7; focus on petitioner — "Alas, I am a widow," 2 Sam 14:5; and background of the problem — use of the perfect tense), it must be recognized that this is the most *particular* of the elements so far listed (it being the main thing which differentiates one case from the other). As this section involves the vocabulary of vocalization only once (2 Sam 19:29) and as it is no different in form from similar sections in other legal proceedings (see above, 1 Kgs 3:16-28), one here need specify only its *function* in the overall form. Though on the surface this element may appear to be only a simple description of a situation, placed where it is in the overall form, this description functions as a quite specific *petition.* It is a desperate request for judicial decision to which the king is now obligated to respond.

The king — judgment

As the king's judgment is a response to the particular statement of the case described above, it too varies dramatically among the narratives of this section. In light of this fact, and because of the absence of vocalizing vocabulary and similarities with other judicial narratives (see above), only a cursory treatment of this element of the outline will be attempted. Two observations are, however, appropriate.

First, the primary cue for this section is what might be called the "royal imperative" (cf. 1 Kgs 3:24-25). This imperative is present in three of the five narratives (2 Sam 14:8, 2 Kgs 8:6, 2 Sam 19:30). Indeed, so expected is this imperative as a conclusion to a royal procedure that its absence in the two remaining narratives (2 Kgs 6:24-31 and 1 Kgs 20:35-43) is the final deciding clue (following the horror of the case in 2 Kings 6 and the use of disguise and self-incriminating testimony in 1 Kings 20) that something is here amiss (namely the king's failure to trust Elisha, 2 Kings 6, and another king's failure to uphold the ban, 1 Kings 20). The absence of the imperative in these two cases is therefore *not* a rejection of this form, but a testimony to its fixity — demonstrating the power of recognizable *variations* on this form, both in literature and in life.

Second, it is significant that though matters of life and death are indeed here at stake, all these narratives end not with saving or judging *actions* on the part of the king, but with the king's *speaking* (2 Sam 14:24, 2 Kgs 6:31, 2 Kgs 8:6, 2 Sam 19:30) or, more striking, his *failure to speak* (1 Kgs 20:43). This again highlights the elevated status of the king in this particular setting.

The king, like God, need not *act* to save; the utterance of his words in judgment is enough![14]

Conclusions

While the previous chapter's location of $z'q$ and $s'q$ within their word field enabled some narrowing with regard to their possible range of meanings, the results of this prior analysis combined with those of this chapter allow a considerable increase in precision. *Within this particular setting in life,* one might specify the meaning signified by a choice of $z'q$ or $s'q$ according to the situational categories above: (1) *situation of need* — points toward the particular function of these words as appeals for legal hearing, cries for help whose intensity is grounded in the life and death issues at stake; (2) *identity of the participants* — the tremendous gap separating the widow and the king in terms of legal power indicates the mixture of desperation (given this huge disparity in status), resignation (in terms of any possible change in this relative status), and hope (grounded in the obligation this relational status imposes) with which this cry for help is uttered; and (3) *actual characteristics of the request* — the central position of this cry for help within this five-fold form of personal interaction underlines the absolutely crucial initiatory function this brief, intense, directed, and apparently articulate vocalization performs; interrupting the king in his passing and petitioning him to turn and hear and save.

II. SIMILAR SITUATIONAL SETTINGS OF THE CRY— THE POSSIBILITY OF OVERLAPPING MEANINGS

The precise description of the semantics of the cry of the marginal to the king in the preceding section is attributable to two factors: (1) a remarkable similarity in the vocabulary and syntax of the vocalization, and (2) its location in a relatively fixed social setting ascertainable through five narrative texts in the Old Testament and supporting evidence in the ancient Near East. But what happens when cues of syntax are not so precise and no full form is discernible? How much does the cry, the situation, and/or the identity of the participants need to change before the findings for the particular setting in the first part of this chapter become irrelevant for other settings where similar vocabulary occurs? This question of the "transfer of meaning"[15] is central to many of the

[14] This may help explain the numerous times both the king's and God's judicial function is connected poetically with the more tangible activities of feeding and freeing (e.g., Jer 21:12, Deut 10:18, and Ps 146:7). It is possible, however, that such parallel terms point to two different, but related aspects of "kingship" in relation to the oppressed.

[15] This issue crops up in many shapes and forms in the primary articles on $z'q$ and $s'q$ with which this dissertation is in dialogue: Boecker on the "technical" meaning of $z'q/s'q$ in regard to legal procedure, in *Redeformen*, pp. 62–63; Albertz' rejection of this particular meaning of $z'q/s'q$ as the "original" meaning from which all others should be derived,

conclusions of the next chapter. Therefore, it will be dealt with here in a preliminary way with regard to several texts less central to the final conclusions of this dissertation.

The Cry of the Oppressed (Exod 22:20-23; cf. Deut 15:9 and 24:15)

In the midst of the Book of the Covenant, the verb $s\,^{\varsigma}q$ is used to describe the cry of an oppressed widow or orphan to God. That this use of the cry has much in common with the cry of the marginal to the king might be demonstrated as follows:

Cues of syntax

That this is a cry "for help" is indicated by: (1) the use of the directional preposition ('elay, v 22), (2) its emphatic linkage (through paired infinitive absolutes) with the vocabulary of "response" (šm ', v 22); and (3) the use of similarly "directed" verbs for vocalization in roughly analogous legal contexts (cf. qr' with 'el in Deut 15:9 and 24:15).

Cues of situation

That this cry "for help" is set in a situation analogous to that of the marginal's appeal to the king is indicated by: (1) *the situation of need*—though the situation is only loosely described as one of oppression ('nh, v 21), the following cues point toward the more immediate necessity as "legal hearing"; (2) *the identity of the participants*—here are two of those legally classified "marginals" (the widow and the orphan, 'almānâ wĕyātôm, v 21) immediately preceded by the third (the resident alien, gēr, v 20); and (3) *actual characteristics of the request*—though the full form is not present (as is to be expected in a legal code versus a narrative), its general pattern is: (a) approach of marginal—the cry (v 22b); (b) reply of king—"I will surely hear them" (v 22c); and (c) king's judgment—the retributive verdict: wives and children of oppressors will themselves become legally destitute, i.e., widows and orphans (v 23).

All the above cues argue for a quite close syntactical and situational link (between this use of $s\,^{\varsigma}q$ and that in the preceding section) and hence for a fairly

---

THAT 2:572; and Hasel's tentative assertions regarding the intersection of the "socio-legal" and "religio-theological" semantic spheres for $z\,^{\varsigma}q/s\,^{\varsigma}q$, *TDOT* 4:117. It should be noted that no "diachronic" arguments for meaning are here being made—i.e., this chapter does *not* posit an original meaning in the setting of the marginal's cry to the king from which other meanings are then "derived" (cf. arguments based on "Zetergeschrei" or "Zeterruf" of von Rad, etc., cited above, n. 5). It simply points to a remarkable precision of meaning in one setting of $z\,^{\varsigma}q/s\,^{\varsigma}q$'s wide-ranging use and asks what other settings of the cry might share in this particular semantic precision, using previously discovered cues of syntax and situation.

large semantic "overlap" (with the conclusions of that section). However, there are two essential differences with regard to the "identity of the participants" which will become much more important in the next chapter:

God versus the king

The judge in this passage is no longer the earthly, but the heavenly king. Though the continuity of vocabulary and form as one moves from the marginal's appeal to the king to these same marginals' appeals to God is both striking and significant (cf. the similarity of posture and gesture discussed above), it is not surprising, given the social world of ancient Israel. One of the essential traits shared by both the human and the divine king is a special responsibility for the legally powerless (e.g., Deut 10:18; Jer 49:11; Mal 3:5, Pss 68:5 and 146:9). It is therefore to be expected that the marginal in need of legal decision would "approach" the king and God in similar ways.

The "oppressed" versus the "marginal"

Immediately following these particular verses in the Covenant Code are similar laws regarding the receipt of interest and securities from the "poor" ('ammî, v 24) and one's "neighbor" (rēa', v 25)—replete with the verb ṣ'q and the directional preposition 'el (yiṣ'aq ēlay, v 26). Though this broadening of the class of the marginals to include the "poor," the "needy," and the "oppressed" (e.g., dāl, 'ebyôn, 'ānî) is common in the Old Testament (Deut 15:9 and 24:15 as well as Jer 22:3, 16; Zech 7:10; Ps 82:3; Ps 72:4 and 12-14), it is nonetheless problematic for the situational arguments of this chapter. Much of the preceding argument regarding the legal aspects of the cry of the marginal to the king hinged on the particular *legal* relationship binding these specific "marginals" and the king. Though one may well posit a spectrum of precariousness before the law, as one shifts to categories of more general poverty and/or oppression, the particular "situation of need" and "characteristics of the request" will necessarily receive much more weight in deciding for or against any *legal* nuances of the cry—as will be demonstrated in the two remaining texts in this chapter.

The Cry of the Raped (Deut 22:23-27; cf. Gen 39:14, 15, 18 and 2 Sam 13:19)

In the legal material of Deuteronomy, the verb ṣ'q is used to describe the cry of a betrothed virgin who is the victim of rape in the city (Deut 22:24) versus the country (Deut 22:27). Though this vocalization undoubtedly indicates the cry of a woman in dire straits—a cry which has obvious legal implications in the social structures of Israel—it must be contrasted with the cry of the marginal to the king in the following ways.

Cues of syntax

Syntactically, there is a fundamental ambiguity regarding the function of this cry. *On the one hand,* certain cues indicate this cry's function as a cry "of pain" (arising out of physical and/or emotional trauma): (1) its undirected nature (*bā'ir*, v 24, and *baśśādeh*, v 27, provide only the "locus" of the cry); (2) similar undirected cries in *narratives* concerning rape (e.g., *wā'eqrā' běqôl gādôl*, Gen 39:14 — which functions only to cause the purported rapist to flee, not to summon help; cf. "she summoned the men of the household," *qr'* plus direct object with *lĕ*, at the beginning of the verse); and (3) a similar undirected use of *z'q* follwing the rape of Tamar (2 Sam 13:19) whose accompaniment by the gestures and posture of mourning (ashes, rent clothes, hand on head) indicate its function as a cry of lamentation over the loss of her virginity. *On the other hand,* certain cues indicate this cry's function as a cry "for help" (indicating hope for intervention and/or witnesses in response): (1) the inappropriateness of a directed cry for such an omnidirectional appeal for help (i.e., to anyone in city or country within earshot); (2) the explicit linkage of the second cry (v 27) with the assumed absence of a "savior," *môšîa'* (whose "response" — intervention, later testimony, etc. — is left ambiguous); and (3) the "natural" (and possibly "pan-cultural") expectation regarding the purpose of such a cry if voiced *during* (as in this passage) as opposed to *after* (as in 2 Samuel 13) such a crime. The "at-odds" nature of these syntactical cues force one to turn to situational cues for clarification.

Cues of situation

Here the evidence is less ambiguous. Though any precise cues of form are absent, cues for the remaining situational categories are not: (1) *situation of need.* Though it is true that this cry later possesses legal implications of life and death proportions, it is hard to believe that such legal necessities explain its initial utterance. In the mouth of the virgin being raped, this cry is not an appeal for legal hearing, but a cry of a more immediate kind (either non-directed "in pain" or directed "for help"). (2) *identity of the participants.* Though the virgin is a woman and hence a person of limited legal rights, she is not a "marginal" in the strictest sense (indeed, v 24 signals her decided "male-connectedness by designating her *iśśāh* or "wife"), nor need her "savior" be a king (but only anyone who can hear her cry and respond in the role of "savior"). If this woman cries out to another, she does so *not* on the basis of assumed inequalities of judicial power, but on the basis of inequalities of a more inclusive kind (such as those of physical strength or the "disinterest" necessary for later testimony).

Therefore, regardless of whether one interprets this cry as primarily a cry "for help" (making the key question of law the presence or absence of someone to intervene in the assault) or a cry "of pain" (shifting the question to the presence or absence of a witness to the virgin's lack of consent), the above situational cues point away from any close semantic link between this cry and the cry of the marginal to the king. This is not a cry for legal appeal, but a more ambiguous outcry in the midst of rape which only *later* is of extraordinary significance in court.

The Cry of the Blood (Gen 4:10; cf. Ps 9:13)

In the Yahwistic story of Cain and Abel, the verb ṣʿq is used to describe the crying of Abel's blood to God (Gen 4:10). At first glance, given several explicable shifts in syntax and the "identity of the participants," this use of the cry seems closely analogous to the cry of the marginal to the king. Again, various cues might be listed:

Cues of syntax

That this is a cry "for help" is indicated by: (1) the use of the directional preposition ('elay, v 10); and (2) its placement in the narrative (cited as the cause of God's "response," i.e., the questioning of Cain, v 10). The only shift here is one of verbal forms—instead of a finite form of the verb, this passage uses a participle, ṣōʿăqîm (v 4). This contrast between the brief outcry of the marginal and the ongoing wail of the blood probably has less to do with the "for help" function of the cry than with the particular characteristics of this cry's subject, i.e., the blood (cf. Job's wish that his blood find no resting place, Job 16:18). The blood of the murdered innocent does not cry out once and stop; it characteristically keeps on crying out until it is heard (cf. the literary device of the "wandering spirit").

Cues of situation

That this cry "for help" is set in a situation analogous to that of the marginal's appeal to the king is indicated by: (1) *the situation of need.* The need here is not actually that of the blood, but of that person whose life this blood now "represents," i.e , Abel. Abel, now dead, can obviously not represent himself at the trial of his own murder. It is therefore left to his blood to appeal for such a hearing, a "testimonial" function elsewhere in evidence (e.g., Job 16:18–19—note the link between the cry of the blood and talk of a prospective "witness" or "advocate," ʿēd and śāhēd). (2) *identity of the participants.* As with the cry of the raped, one must distinguish between a cry *during* a crime and a cry which *follows.* During a murder, the victim, like the raped virgin, may well cry out in a decidedly "immediate" fashion (e.g., in physical pain or for physical intervention). But following a murder, as is the case here, the cry functions in a more "technical," if no less "necessary" way—i.e., as a cry for *vengeance.* Directed toward the murdered's kin, this is a cry for vengeance on a personal and individual level; i.e., for an "avenger of the blood," gōʾēl haddām (Num 35:19; Deut 19:6; Josh 20:3; etc.). But if this murder occurs in the fields (baśśādeh, v 8), or for some reason it is necessary to cry toward the king or God, then this is a cry for vengeance on a more comprehensive or "judicial" level, i.e., that the system of blood vengeance itself be preserved (as in such narratives as 2 Sam 4:1–12 and 2 Kgs 9:1–37, concerning the king and God respectively, especially 2 Sam 4:11 and 2 Kgs 9:7). Here it seems is a special type of legal appeal properly directed toward the king or God, an appeal they both were especially obligated to hear (cf. Ps 72:14 and Ps 9:13). (3) *the actual characteristics of the request.* Though, as with the cry of the oppressed above, the entire form is not present, the general pattern is: (a) approach of marginal—the cry of the blood (v 10); (b) reply of king—evidenced in God's turning to Cain to inquire after Abel (vv 9 and 10); and (c) judgment of king—"therefore now you are cursed . . ." (vv 11–12 and 15; note the repeated use of the modal imperfect—*tōsep, tēt, tihĕyeh, yuqqām*—to signal a command). All the above cues argue for a quite close syntactical, situational, and hence semantic link between the more inclusive cry of the marginal for legal appeal (which may include issues of blood vengeance, 2 Sam 14:11) and this more particular appeal of the blood on behalf of the murdered.

However, there yet remains a shift of emphasis in this narrative which must not be overlooked. While the cry in the five narratives in the first half of this chapter came at the center of a "process" between the king and the marginal her- or himself, the cry in this story is referred to secondarily as the motivation for another closely related "process" now unfolding, i.e., that between the king as judge and a relevant "third" party—in this case, the murderer, Cain. This slight shift in situational context may be linked to a shift in literary context (from that of DtrH and the legal codes of Exodus and Deuteronomy to that of the Yahwist) with further implications for the semantics of this particular "cry of the blood." Such questions of the relationship between literary context and meaning are the topic of the next chapter.

4
The Setting in Literature

On the one hand, certain features of sentences which contain this expression appear to remain constant and as such to be independent of any particular literary setting. . . . On the other hand, certain other features of the sentences appear to be directly related to the particular literary setting in which they occur. . . . The question to which the study must now turn is: to what extent are these stylistic differences indicative of a difference in the semantic function of the phrase in its various literary settings?

Balentine on the phrase "hide the face,"
in *The Hidden God,* pp. 46–49.

For readers of the English Bible, the next step might seem obvious. Having honed their awareness of the semantic possibilities of the verb "cry" within its word field, and having discovered its repeated use within a particular setting-in-life in the social world of ancient Israel, they might now attempt to discuss the significance of its choice to describe that "cry" which the sentence "then we cried to the Lord" most consistently brings to mind: the cry of the slaves in Egypt. In terms of word choice and situational context, the chance for semantic similarities appears great indeed.

It is the premise of this chapter that here the reader of Hebrew would and should again do the same. The repeated choice of directed forms of $z^{\epsilon}q$ or $s^{\epsilon}q$ in sentences such as *wanniṣ'aq 'el-yhwh* (Num 20:16), *wanniṣ'aq 'el-yhwh 'ĕlōhê 'ăbōtênû* (Deut 26:7), and *wayyiṣ'āqû 'el-yhwh* (Josh 24:7) has already been mentioned. Just as important is the linkage of this particular group of "slaves" in Egypt with that class of legal "marginals," the resident alien (*gēr,* Exod 23:9, Lev 19:33–34; Deut 10:19 and 24:17–18), who—like the orphan and widow—could "cry out" ($z^{\epsilon}q$ or $s^{\epsilon}q$) to God when "oppressed" (Exod 22:20–23; cf. *'nh*-pi, vv 21 and 22 and Exod 1:11–12).[1] The question of overlapping

---

[1] This link between the oppression of the resident alien and the crying out of the widow and orphan may be closer than the present text of Exodus 22 indicates. See the proposed rearrangement (20a, 22b, 21, 22a, and 23) in Childs, *Exodus,* pp. 449–50. Furthermore, the linkage of the legal status of such "marginals" and that of slaves is common elsewhere in the ancient Near East. For example, note the following instructions for the commander of the Hittite border guards: "Whenever you arrive at a town, call all the people of the town together. For him who has a complaint, judge it and set him right. If a *man's slave* or a man's *slave-girl* or a *widowed woman* has a complaint [against someone] judge it for them and set them right . . ." (*ANET,* p. 211, italics mine).

meanings between the cry of the marginal to the king and the cry of the slaves to God is thus quite unavoidable and serves as the starting point for the various sections of this chapter.

The only danger is that one might here leave the careful analyses of syntax and situation used in the preceding chapters and begin to treat this "cry of the slaves" as if it were a one-dimensional vocalization to which previous conclusions might now be uniformly "applied." While the overriding *similarities* between the "historical summaries" above might point one in such a direction, as previously noted (beginning of Chapter 3), they possess other difficulties for interpretation which preclude their analysis from being central. But when one turns to those primary texts at the beginning of Exodus where this "cry of the slaves" is first recorded (at least canonically),[2] various essential *differences* in the way this cry is recounted demonstrate both the inappropriate and limited nature of such a "univocal" approach.

Therefore, this chapter will examine the cry of the slaves in Egypt as recorded by each of the major Pentateuchal sources in God's words of promise to Moses (J—Exod 3:7-8; E—Exod 3:9-10; and P—Exod 6:2-8)[3] as well as the introductory "cry" provided by the latest of these (P—Exod 2:23b-25).[4] The goal of this examination will be to link shifts in vocabulary, syntax, and form to shifts in the overall "conceptual frameworks"[5] within which these various literary

[2] The possibility of the temporal priority of the more formal "capsule" recollections of the communal cry (such as the historical summaries listed above) will be alluded to briefly at the beginning of the next chapter.

[3] The consensus of various scholars on the identification of the literary sources for these passages is quite remarkahle, making this an almost "textbook" example for the source-critical method. For example, see J. Estlin Carpenter and G. Harford-Battersby, eds., *The Hexateuch according to the Revised Version*, 2 vols. (London: Longmans, Green, and Co., 1900) 1: 29–30 and 2: 82–83, 87; Schmidt, *Exodus*, II/2: 95–98, 106–9; Childs, *Exodus*, pp. 28, 52–53, 111–114; Martin Noth, *Exodus: A Commentary*, The Old Testament Library (Philadelpha: Westminster Press, 1962), pp. 33–35, 59–62; Plastaras, *Exodus*, pp. 58–59, 66–74; and J. P. Hyatt, *Exodus*, New Century Bible Commentary (Grand Rapids: William B. Eerdmans Publishing Co., 1971), p. 48.

[4] Neither precise dating nor final conclusions on the independent redactional status of the P material in Exodus is essential for the arguments of this chapter. Compare Noth, *Exodus*, p. 16; Plastaras, *Exodus*, p. 19; Hyatt, *Exodus*, p. 25; and Brevard S. Childs, *Introduction to the Old Testament as Scripture* (Philadelpha: Fortress Press, 1979), pp. 122–23, 162, 172–73. However, in broad terms, these sources are assumed to be arranged chronologically as: J (circa 950 B.C.), E (935–721 B.C.), and P (exilic; see Plastaras, *Exodus*, pp. 15–19), with the P school providing the final framework for the narrative as a whole. Such a view is supported by the "framing" function of Exod 2:23b-25 and 6:2-8 for this portion of the narrative, as noted in Plastaras, *Exodus*, p. 19. The primary distinction between the groups of passages as listed is three *parallel* versions of God's words of promise to Moses versus one *non-parallel* version which serves as the "introduction" for them all.

[5] Terminology becomes an increasing problem at this point. The term "conceptual

sources understand and appropriate this cry. These conceptual frameworks may then be compared with other literary contexts demonstrating a similar use of the cry.

I. THE CRY IN GOD'S WORDS OF PROMISE TO MOSES

The Cry in Exod 3:7-8

And Yahweh said, "I have indeed seen the affliction of my people who are in Egypt and their outcry on account of their taskmasters I have heard. Surely, I know their sufferings. So I have come down to deliver them from the hand of the Egyptians and to bring them up out of that land to a good and broad land, to a land flowing with milk and honey, to the place of the Canaanites, the Hittites, the Amorites, the Perizzites, the Hivites, and the Jebusites (Exod 3:7-8).

The cry in the J traditions

Viewed strictly within the context of the J materials in the opening chapters of Exodus, one might identify Exod 3:7-8 as the "promise" following upon "the discovery of a holy site" (cf. Gen 28: 11-22; see Schmidt, *Exodus,* II/2: 110-21), a "promise" linked through vocabulary (*'am, 'lh,* etc.) with the Yahwist's introduction in Exod 1:8-14. However, such an analysis does little to explicate the meaning of verses 7 and 8 *themselves*—built around a nominal form of the cry (*saʿăqâ*) and the "seeing, hearing, knowing, and coming down" of God (*r'h, šmʿ, ydʿ,* and *yrd*). For this, the use of the cry in two prior narratives from the J material, Gen 4:10 and Gen 18:20, 21, are instructive.

(1) *The cry of the blood in the story of Cain and Abel, Gen 4:10.* In the concluding section of the last chapter, both the continuity of this "cry of the blood" with the cry of the marginal to the king (in terms of its "judicial" function) and its discontinuity with the same (in terms of participants: God and third party) were discussed. It remains here to analyze this qualified overlap in terms of its setting in literature, i.e., the J portion of the primeval history.

Beginning with the rebellion of Adam and Eve in Genesis 3 and their subsequent expulsion from the garden, the Yahwist recounts a series of stories of "crime and punishment" demonstrating the various ways both individuals (3:1-24; 4:3-16) and communities (6:1-4, [6:5-9:17, includes P material], 11:1-9) revolt as creatures against the creator (Westermann, *Genesis 1-11,* pp. 18 and 53). Within this context, the actions of God in response to these crimes by human beings may be properly designated as "judicial" (Westermann, *Genesis 1-11,* p. 303) and collectively schematized as follows: (a) *"the verification of the facts of the case"* — evidence of revolt comes before God the judge either by "hearing"

---

framework" is meant to include, but point beyond the more limited syntagmatic and form-critical distinctions of chapters 2 and 3 to the collection of concepts and ideas within which the cry's meaning must be discussed. Roughly analogous are the "contextual settings" of Balentine, *The Hidden God,* p. 49, and the "set-piece styles" of Sawyer, *Semantics,* p. 29.

(*šm'* —implicit, Gen 4:10) or "seeing" (*r'h* —Gen 6:5 and 11:5) to which God responds by "coming down" (*yrd* —Gen 11:5) to see and hear more closely, to investigate the veracity of the testimony so far received (especially through the use of questions and answers —Gen. 3:9-13 and 4:9-10); and (b) "the sentence" —upon confirming the case against the individual or the community, God the judge then pronounces his sentence (Gen 3:14-19; 4:11-12, 15; 6:3; 6:7; 11:7), following which the relevant judicial actions (Gen 3:23-24; 4:15b; 11:8) and results (Gen 4:16; 6:4; 11:9; and the whole of the flood story) are recounted.[6]

Within this judicial form, the function of the single use of *z'q* or *s'q* in the primeval history is quite straightforward. The scene has now shifted from the initial appeal of the "marginal" —in this case the cry of the blood of Abel, murdered in the fields —to the resulting investigation by the judge particularly responsible for such undisclosed crimes against the innocent —God himself. Thus, while the cry may yet function implicitly as an initiatory appeal for legal hearing, its primary function *within this narrative* of crime and punishment is *evidential* —serving as the rationale for a "trial" which is now in progress. Given this shift in narrative function, one might expect a shift in syntax —perhaps from verbal to nominal forms. Here the participle (*ṣō'ăqîm*, v 10), though a "verbal noun,"[7] may well be more the exception than the rule —due again to the peculiar nature of its subject (the blood —see last chapter) and perhaps to the heightened immediacy such a form implies (i.e., instead of "I have heard the cry of your brother Abel's blood," "*even now,* as you, Cain, speak, the voice of your brother's blood *is crying to me* from the ground").

(2) *The cry of Sodom and Gomorrah, Gen 18:20, 21.* Though no longer within the narratives of the primeval history, and though the third party in this trial is not the accused but an intercessor pleading on the accused's behalf (Abraham, 18:22-33), there is no doubt that this passage shares both the legal provenance and the basic structure of the "crime and punishment" narratives above. Here the *setting of judicial procedure* is even more clearcut —given Abraham's "standing" before God (*'md,* 18:10 —see above; or God's standing before Abraham, *Tiq soph*), his "drawing near" (*ngš,* 18:23; cf. Isa 41:22), and his reference to God as the "judge of all the earth" (*šōpēṭ, 18:25) —if the two-fold structure* slightly less so —the verification of the facts of the case (18:16-32) and the sentence (19:1-29, especially v 13). Nevertheless, within this narrative as a whole, the function of the cry seems quite consistent.

Again, this story deals with a crime the punishment of which is the particular responsibility of either the king or God. This is not the more narrow, if no less heinous crime of violated sexual norms —to which a restricted focus on certain vocabulary might lead (e.g., *yd'* —19:5; cf. Judg 19:22, 25, and *nēbālâ* —

---

[6] For these headings, see Plastaras, *Exodus,* p. 71. Here he uses these headings to compare the structure of God's words of promise to Moses with that of prophetic oracles.

[7] Ronald J. Williams, *Hebrew Syntax: An Outline,* 2d ed. (Toronto: University of Toronto Press, 1976) p. 39.

Judg 19:24; cf. Gen 34:7). Rather it is the broader, and more fundamental question of how a city treats its resident aliens (*qerîm,* Lot in Gen 19:9; the old man in Judg 19:16), particularly with regard to their right to harbor guests (the two angels in Gen 19:1, the Levite in Judg 19:1). That this is the case is supported by the way the prophetic traditions broaden the sin of Sodom and Gomorrah to include such diverse crimes as lying, unwillingness to repent, and failure to protect the poor and afflicted (e.g., Jer 23:14 and Ezek 16:49,[8] yet return in more extended passages (Isa 1:10-17) to the more systemic crime of a city's failure to protect its legally marginal, through partiality or lack of concern (Isa 1:17; cf. 1:23 and 3:9). If the princes of a city do not allow the cases of that city's marginals to come to them (*wĕrîb 'almānâ lō'-yābô' 'ălêhem,* Isa 1:23), then God as judge must "take his place to adjudicate (*lārîb),*" must "stand (*wĕ'ōmēd*) in order to judge (*lādîn*) his people" (Isa 3:13). As a king's rule may be judged by his treatment of the marginal, so may a city by its mistreatment of the same.

Given this situational setting and its literary setting within the J material, the specific vocabulary and form of Gen 18:20, 21 fall into place. Here again is that first section of the above judicial procedure, *the verification of the facts of the case:* evidence of wrong-doing has come before God the judge, again (as in Genesis 4), implicitly, by hearing (v 20); to which God responds by going down (*yrd*) to see (*r'h*) and thereby to know (*yd',* cf. Gen 4:9?) whether the "accused" of Sodom and Gomorrah have done (*'śh,* cf. Gen 4:10) altogether according to the evidence which has come to him (v 21). The evidence in this case, as in the case of Cain and Abel above, is the "cry," this time in the expected nominal form (*za'ăqat sĕdōm wa'ămōrâ,* v 20; *hakkĕsa'ăqātāh habbā'â 'elay,* v 21).

In this judicial setting, the choice of *ṣ'q* instead of one of the other vocalizations from its field indicates *semantically* that this is a cry "for help," specifically for legal hearing, arising from the maltreated marginals *within* this community (versus the "clamor" of the wicked, *šĕ'ôn,* Ps 74:23; or the "shout" of destruction, *sĕwāḥa,* Jer 14:2; both of which may go up, *'lh,* from a people or city *as a whole;* cf. the uproar of all humankind in the *Epic of Atrahasis, ANET,* pp. 104–6). In this narrative setting, the use of the nominal form underlines this cry's evidential function, serving as the basis for a "trial" which is either about to begin (Gen 18:20–21) or is already completed (Gen 19:13). This function of the cry as evidence for the prosecution is strengthened in this case by the particular form of the sentence in which it is included. As the person with a complaint must come (*bō'*) before the king (see last chapter), so this negative evidence comes to God (*bō'* plus *'el,* Gen 18:20) and, thereby, becomes great "before" him (*lipnê,* Gen 19:23; cf. 2 Kgs 19:28, Jonah 1:2, Lam 1:22).

Given this background, the vocabulary and form of the promise to Moses in the J material becomes remarkably transparent. The judicial provenance of such words as *r'h, šm', yd',* and *yrd* in the J traditions is now apparent. Their

---

[8] Compare Walter Brueggemann, *Genesis: A Bible Commentary for Teaching and Preaching,* Interpretation (Atlanta: John Knox Press, 1982) p. 164.

arrangement according to the two-fold structure of verification (v 7) and sentence (v 8) differs here only in a curtailment of the "investigation" — so that when God "comes down," he does so not to "see" and "hear" and thereby to "know" more conclusively (cf. Gen 11:5), but in order to judge (cf. Gen 11:7). Finally, here again the cry is a nominal form of $z^{\prime}q$ or $s^{\prime}q$ ($sa^{\prime}\check{a}q\hat{a}$, v 7) indicating, by word choice, its semantic value as an appeal of marginals (the slaves) for help in legal terms, and, by form, its functional value as evidence upon which this judicial proceeding is based.

However, there is one major shift in form which must not be missed and is obviously significant for the later appropriation of this cry by the readers of the J traditions. Heretofore, the Yahwist's narratives have been labeled stories of "crime and punishment." In the larger context of the book of Exodus, this is undoubtedly the case here as well (i.e., the judgment against Pharaoh and the Egyptians for their oppression of the slaves through the destruction of the plagues and the "battle" at the sea). But in the more restricted context of Exod 3:7–8, the appearance of "my people" ('ammî) in verse 7 is a cue that something different is here afoot. More than a story of "crime and punishment" (with a focus on the past trial and sentencing of the accused), this is a story of "crime and promise" (with a focus on the future vindication of the case or "cry" of those who have been wronged).

Again, this shift is no doubt significant and certainly central to the appropriation of this cry by the descendants of these slaves. However, it must not obscure the essential *continuity* of all these cases in the J traditions. The message of these narratives is the same whether God acts in judgment against the accused or salvation for the wronged. God is a righteous king who fulfills his special responsibility to hear the cries of the marginal *for justice* by moving immediately through "due process" to set things right.

The conceptual framework of the cry in the J traditions.

As the above analysis indicates, the use of $z^{\prime}q$ or $s^{\prime}q$ in judicial settings within the J material is both semantically similar (in terms of the nature of the cry) and functionally dissimilar (in terms of its role in the narrative) to the use of the "cry" in the narratives of the marginal's appeal to the king. The nature of this overlap might be characterized according to the following three dimensions:

(1) *Implied contrast.* One way of describing the functional shift in the use of the cry by the Yahwist would be to talk of a move from a "cry to" (indicated by the directed verbal forms in the previous chapter's narratives) to a "cry against" (indicated by the nominal forms in the three J narratives above). This shift is least clear in Genesis 4, where the form is both verbal (a participle) and directed (to God), leaving the "against Cain" function of this cry to the structure of the narrative as a whole. In Genesis 18, the "against" nature of the cry is perhaps more explicit (particularly in Gen 19:13 where the causal connection between the cry and the city's destruction is made clear), but the particular

identity of those thereby condemned (the people of these cities who have caused the cries of the marginals to come to God) slightly less so (hence the recourse to secondary, prophetic sources). However, in Exod 3:7, both the "against" nature of the cry and the identity of those thereby accused are evident in the phrase which contains the cry, i.e., "their cry *on account of their taskmasters*" (*mippĕnê nōgĕśāyw*). In the J framework, once a cry from the marginal has been heard by the king, it functions as a cry *against* his or her murderer (Gen 4:8), assailant (Gen 19:13), or oppressor (Exod 1:11 and 5:6-14).

(2) *No special relationship.* The king in the narratives of the preceding chapter turns to hear the case of the marginal not because of any special relationship between him and this particular individual (note the lack of proper names), but because of his essential royal obligation to respond to any marginal's appeal for justice. Likewise, God does not come down to investigate either the murder of Abel or the legal violations of Sodom and Gomorrah because of any special relationship to Abel ("the voice of *your* brother's blood is crying to me," Gen 4:10) or the violated of those cities ("the cry of Sodom and Gomorrah," Gen 18:20), but because of his general responsibilities as "judge of all the earth" (Gen 18:25). Though the identification of the "criers" in Exod 3:7 as "my people" may begin a shift away from the non-particular nature of this judicial process, one must recognize that this is a shift which is foreign to the framework of the marginal's cry as a whole (note how none of the plural suffixes on *sa'ăqātām, nōgĕśāyw,* or *mak'ōbāyw* fits its singular antecedent, *'ammî*). The "special" thrust of these narratives has much less to do with the particular identity of the crier in relation to the king than with the particular nature of this king's rule itself; i.e., this is a king who does indeed hear and respond, repeatedly, to the cries of the marginal.

(3) *Royal preservation of order.* There is no doubt who is the primary actor in these narratives. Though God looks back on the various cries as the basis for his actions, the repeated initiatives within these narratives are traced not to human beings but to the divine, royal judge (note the repeated use of the first person singular, "*I* have seen," etc.). So consistent is this stress that these stories might better be called narratives of "the royal preservation of order." Both individually and together they serve notice that Yahweh is a king according to the highest standards in the ancient Near East. This king's preservation of order is dramatically contrasted with Pharaoh's failure to do the same, particularly his refusal to hear the cries of the marginals under his rule (Exod 5:15-18 — note here the full use of the previous chapter's form beginning with *wayyiṣ'aqû 'el-par'ōh*). Central to the framework of the cry in the J material is the recognition of the king, i.e., Yahweh, as the one who ensures that this cry for legal hearing functions as it should — setting in motion a judicial procedure which does not falter or fail, leading either to judgment of the accused (e.g., Cain) or salvation of the wronged (e.g., the slaves).

Other literary contexts which share this framework of the cry.

The last chapter is full of passages which share the Yahwist's location of the cry within the general theme of the royal preservation of order (note how each of the five central narratives is actually a "test" of particular kings' ability to provide such order in the judicial sphere; cf. Ps 9:13). It would not be difficult to find other passages which follow the Yahwist's functional shift from a "cry to" to a "cry against" (note the shift from verbal, directed to nominal, undirected forms in Exod 22:22 as one moves from the initial crying for justice to the received cry as basis for impending judgment, v 23; cf. the "cry" of the vineyard in Isa 5:7, which follows the requested judgment in v 3 and the proposed judgment in vv 5 and 6). However, there is a larger literary context which preserves the conceptual framework of the J materials quite precisely, yet asks of it a question the Yahwist does not—what happens when God as judge does *not* respond to the cries of the marginal? Should such an unheard cry be used as evidence in a case against him?

According to the book of Proverbs and the arguments of Elihu in the book of Job, it should not. Both of these maintain that God is yet the legal protector of the marginal (orphan—Prov 23:10-11) and, by extension, the "poor" and "afflicted" (Prov 22:22-23); *their* cries God continues to hear (Job 34:28b— *wĕsaʿăqat ʿăniyyîm yišmāʿ*). However, if another person's cry goes unheard, they should not complain. Either they have shut their ears from the cry of the poor (Prov 21:13—*mizzaʿăqat-dāl*) and hence they call out (*yiqrāʾ*) and God does not answer (*wĕlōʾ yēʿāneh*); or they have actually caused such cries to come before God (Job 34:28a—*lĕhābîʾ ʿālāyw saʿăqat-dāl;* cf. Gen 18:21) and hence God regards their cries not as legitimate appeals for justice, but "empty cries" (Job 35:13—*šāwʾ*) which he surely will not hear (*lōʾ-yišmaʿ ʾēl*). Such unheard cries are therefore not testimony against a God who does not fulfill his judicial obligations, but against a person who violates society's most fundamental test of justice, i.e., the protection of the marginal.

Job rejects such an argument forthwith. As a result, Job *does* bring God to trial. Job's "case" against God might be summarized as follows: (1) First, he accepts the premise of the arguments of Proverbs and Elihu by acknowledging God's right to refuse the cries of the wicked (*sʿq*, 27:9). *If* he has mistreated the marginal (see especially 31:13, 16-17, 18-21; cf. 31:32 with Gen 19:1-28), then Job has already pronounced his own curse (31:38-40; note negative cry of the land, *tizʿāq ʿālay*). But, instead, Job has "sat" like a chief, has dwelt like a king among his troops (29:25)—delivering the poor who cried (*šwʿ*, 29:12a) and the orphan who had no helper (*ʿzr*, 29:12b), making the widow's heart sing for joy (29:13b). Job's exercise of judicial power as one of the elders of his community has been far from negligent; indeed it approaches that of the divine judge himself— clothed in justice and righteousness, serving as eyes to the blind and feet to the lame, he who searched out the cause of him or her he did not know (29:14-16). (2) But now without a family, destitute and outcast, Job claims the status of "marginal" for himself. His protected guests, the resident aliens (*gārê bêtî,*

19:15a), have forgotten him. His female slaves count him an alien (*zār*, 19:15b). Indeed, he has become like a stranger (*nokrî*, 9:15c), like a marginal in their eyes (cf. Ps 69:9). His is the status of an Abel (cf. 16:18) or a Lot (see above), one whose cry can be directed to and should be heard by God. (3) The primary evidence against God is thus Job's unheard "cry": "Behold, I cry out, 'Violence!' (*'eṣ'aq hāmās*), but I am not answered (*wĕlō'-'ē'āneh*); I shout for help (*'ăšawwa'*), but there is no justice" (*wĕ'ên mišpāṭ*, Job 19:7). Given Job's past performance as judge and present status as marginal, this unheard "cry" becomes the key evidence for the prosecution of his case against God. Job uses the framework of the cry shared with the J traditions to argue against the king at the center of this framework—God himself, the judge of all the earth.

The Cry in Exod 3:9–12

"And now, behold, the cry of the Israelites has come to me. Moreover, I have seen the oppression with which the Egyptians oppress them. Come now, I will send you to Pharaoh so that you may bring forth my people, the Israelites, from Egypt." But Moses said to God, "Who am I that I should go to Pharaoh and lead out the Israelites from Egypt?" He said, "But I will be with you; and this will be the sign for you that I have sent you: when you have brought forth the people from Egypt, you shall worship God upon this mountain" (Exod 3:9–12).

The cry within the call narratives

There can be little doubt that, at its core, the cry in God's words of promise to Moses in the E materials shares the same essential conceptual framework as that described in the J materials above. Here again is the "seeing" of evidence of wrong-doing (*wĕgam-rā'îtî 'et-hallaḥas*—3:9). Here again, the cry appears in a nominal form (*sa'ăqat bĕnê-yiśrā'ēl*— 3:9). Most important, here again is the specific form of the evidential cry "coming up" to God (*sa'ăqat bĕnê-yiśrā'ēl bā'â 'ēlay*—3:9). God is once again the judge who gathers the evidence in a criminal case concerning the abuse of marginals and moves to respond.

It is, however, in the *mechanics* of this judicial response that signs of a significant difference in the framework of the cry appear. God, the judge, does not "come down" (*yrd*) either to investigate or carry out the sentence. Instead, he "sends" (*šlḥ*) a representative, Moses, to implement the sentence in his stead. As the subjects of the succession of "exodus" verbs demonstrate (*wĕhôṣē'*, 3:10 [note the *LXX*]; *'ôṣî'*, 3:11; and *bĕhôṣî'ăkā*, 3:12), it is the person sent by God, rather than God himself, who will play the central role in the outworking of the divine decision which follows.

The precise function of the cry in the words of promise in the E materials is thus best understood *not* within the Yahwist's structure of "verification" and "sentence," but within a literary genre not limited to the rather tenuously identified E traditions in the book of Exodus (cf. Hyatt, *Exodus,* pp. 21, 22–23, 30–32; Plastaras, *Exodus,* pp. 16–17). This is the genre of the call-form (or "Berufungsformular"; Schmidt, *Exodus,* pp. 123–29) which, placed alongside such comparative texts as Judg 6:11-24 and 1 Sam 9-10, might be described as follows: (1) *the commission* ("Auftrag")—Exod 3:10; Judg 6:14;(1 Sam 9:16); (2) *the protest* ("Einwand")—Exod 3:11; Judg 6:15; 1 Sam 9:21; (3) *the answering of the protest* ("Abweisung des Einwands")—Exod 3:12; Judg 6:16; and (4) *the sign* ("Zeichen")—Exod 3:12; Judg 6:17-21; 1 Sam 10:2-8.

Most important for the function of the cry within this genre is its location in one of this "call-form's" supplemental elements labeled the *grounds* (or "Begrundung," Schmidt, *Exodus,* p. 127) for the call of a savior or deliverer. To this section of the genre belong: (1) *Judg 6:13*—where Gideon contrasts God's past deliverance of the Israelites from Egypt with his present handing over of the Israelites to the Midianites; (2) *1 Sam 9:16*—which relates God's "seeing" of the suffering of his people (*rā'îtî 'et-'ammî;* cf. the *LXX,* which provides the object of God's seeing—*tēn tapeinōsin*) and this people's cry "coming up" to him (*bā'â ṣa'ăqātô 'ēlay*); and (3) *Exod 3:9*—where the content and form (see above) are virtually identical with 1 Sam 9:16.

In the J materials, the cry served a negative evidential function, being the "grounds" for God's initiation and carrying out of a legal procedure leading to judgment and/or salvation. The cry in the E materials serves a similar negative evidential function, but this time through being the "grounds" for God's sending of another savior or deliverer who will rescue in God's stead those who cry out. Though perhaps a slight shift in narrative terms, this leads to some quite significant changes in the conceptual framework of the cry.

The conceptual framework of the cry in the call narratives.

As with the use of $z'q$ and $s'q$ in the J materials, so their use in the call narratives is both semantically similar to (i.e., a cry for help) and functionally dissimilar from (i.e., in terms of a role in the narrative) the use of the "cry" in the narratives of the marginal's appeal to the king. Here the nature of this overlap might again be characterized according to three complementary dimensions.

(1) *Implied summons.* Viewed in terms of its role within these narratives as a whole, the cry here functions not so much as an appeal for legal decision or a cry against those to be prosecuted as a summons to a person sent by God who might save or deliver the "crier(s)" from their distress. Whether this person is Moses (Exodus 3—whose "vocational identity" is difficult to define—see below), Gideon (Judges 6—a judge in a military sense), or Saul (1 Samuel 9—a king in a "transitional" sense), this person's narrative function is the same. This time it concerns not so much the weighing of the pros and cons of a case, as implementing (through various means) a "decision" which God, the judge, has already made.

(2) *Participants particularized.* While the participants in the previous framework were God on the one hand and any person(s) who might be classified as legally "marginal" on the other, the participants here become more varied, yet more particular. In addition to the savior or deliverers listed above, both the

"criers" (*bĕnê-yiśrā'ēl*—Exod 3:9; *bĕnê-yiśrā'ēl*—Judg 6:7; and *'ammî*—1 Sam 9:16) and those from whose hands they would be delivered (*mimmisrāyîm*—Exod 3:10; *mikkaf midyān*—Judg 6:14; and *miyyad pĕlištîm*—1 Sam 9:16) are explicitly identified. Though one might yet limit the *central* "special relationship" in these narratives to that between God and the person God sends ("I will be with *you*," second person singular, Exod 3:10; cf. Judg 6:14), the somewhat awkward shift of the Yahwist away from general legal categories (*'ammî*, Exod 3:7) here goes further. The cry arises in these narratives not from *any* marginal, or even *any* group of people who are oppressed, but from a person or people with a name who would be delivered from others with a name.

(3) *Prophetic disruption of order.* God came down in the J framework to restore order to a system which had been disrupted by revolt on an individual or community level. Like the marginal who cried out to the king, the person(s) who cried out to God in the J material desired pre-eminently that the system would work as it should—punishing those guilty of innocent blood, of violation of the marginal, of maltreatment of slaves (see section on "An Ordering of Rank" in previous chapter). Though perhaps undetectable in the promise to Moses in the E material, the cries in other call narratives often appeal for change of a more radical or revolutionary nature. One person or people must be delivered or saved (*yṣ'*: Exod 3:10, 11, 12; *yš'*-hif: Judg 6:14, 15; 1 Sam 9:16); another put down or destroyed (as the military narratives following Judges 6 and 1 Samuel 9 make clear). These cries push beyond a return to the legal status quo, toward liberation on a wider, less structured scale. Whether or not it is proper to designate this tendency toward disruption "prophetic" (in contrast to the "royal" preservation of order above) is the central concern of the following section.

Other literary contexts which share this framework of the cry

In the E framework of the cry, God, the royal judge, sits at a distance. At the center of the call narratives, and stories of "judgment" which follow, stands that person sent by God—who serves narratively as the instrument by which Yahweh accomplishes the deliverance of those who cry out. The major thrust of this section is to demonstrate the "prophetic" versus "royal" stance of this person or persons in literary contexts which share this general framework of the cry.

(1) *Moses.* In the E materials in Exodus, Moses' status as a wonder-worker over against the king of Egypt and other kings, such as Amalek, is demonstrated by the repeated acts of deliverance he performs, especially through the raising of his rod (cf. von Rad, *Old Testament Theology*, 1:292–93). What may seem unusual, however, is the combination of this role vis-a-vis foreign kings, with other "vocational" cues which point toward Moses' identity as "prophet" (e.g., the nature of his call and sending, and its combination with the revelation of God's name—see Childs, *Exodus*, pp. 55–56, 67–69; cf. Deut 18:15–22, 34:10, and Hos 12:13). It is the *combination* of Moses' interventionist role in the Exodus narratives and the apparent prophetic provenance of the E traditions in general

which leads Gerhard von Rad to classify Moses as a prophet of a "special type —
he is much more the prophet of action, taking an active hand in the events, and
doing so not only through the directions which he gives, but also, and supremely,
by means of dramatic miracles" (von Rad, *Old Testament Theology*, p. 293). As
such, Moses may well serve as the model for the "raising up" (*qôm*-hif) of the
various non-royal "saving" figures who follow (cf. Deut 18:15, 18).

(2) *The Judges*. In the book of Judges, one enters a time when Israel was
explicitly without a king (Judg 21:25). Thus it is not surprising that several
essentially "royal" functions — particularly that of "judging" (see the summary
verb, *špt*, in Judg 10:1-5 and 12:8-15; cf. 1 Sam 8:20) — are here combined with
vocations identified by the writers of this material as "prophetic" (such as that
of Deborah in Judg 4:4-5; cf. Exod 18:13-26 and 2 Sam 15:2-6). What is
surprising, however, is that even the careers of the "saving" judges (versus the
"administrative" judges listed in Judges 10 and 12 above), though also
characterized as "judging" (e.g., Judg 3:10), are yet placed within a general
outline of call and sending which, like that of Moses in Exodus 3, is perhaps best
characterized as "prophetic." Here again the Israelites (*běnê-yiśrā'ēl*, the consistent subjects of the "cry" in this so-called Deuteronomistic formula) cry out to
God (*wayyiz'ăqû 'el-yhwh*, e.g., Judg 3:9, 15) on the grounds of which God then
"raises up" (*qôm*-hif, e.g. Judg 3:9, 15) or "sends" (*šlḥ*, e.g. Judg 6:8, 14 — note
the separation here of the explicitly prophetic and subsequent "saving" figures)
a "savior" (characterized in Judg 3:9 and 15 by the term *môšîa'*, cf. the appeal
of the marginal in 2 Sam 14:4 and 2 Kgs 6:26, *hôšî'â*) who delivers them (signaled
either by a verb — e.g., *wayyôšî'ēm*, Judg 3:9 — or a narrative — e.g., Judg 3:16-30)
from the hands of a foreign king (Cushanrishathaim in Judg 3:10; Eglon in Judg
3:15). There can be little doubt that the Deuteronomistic historian here places
the careers of the various "saving" judges of Israel *within* a framework of the
cry with "prophetic" overtones and *over against* any career or framework which
might be labeled "royal" (note Gideon's explicit refusal of such a vocation, Judg
8:22-23).

(3) *King versus prophet*. An explicit contrast between the career of a person
properly designated as "prophet" and that of a non-foreign (i.e., Israelite) king
awaits that portion of the Deuteronomistic history which serves as the literary
context for all five of the central narratives in the preceding chapter. Here the
"sending" of Israel's first king in response to their cries under foreign oppression
(1 Sam 9:16) is set in juxtaposition with the earlier "sending" of Moses and Aaron
(1 Sam 12:8) and those later "saving" judges mentioned above, up to and
including Samuel (1 Sam 12:11), whose call narrative serves as an introduction
to this particular block of material (1 Sam 3:1-18) and whose role as "judge"
(1 Sam 7:15-17 and 12:1-5; cf. 8:1-3) secures his position in this long line of
"saving" figures. That the establishment of the monarchy in Israel thus placed
in opposition two similar, yet fundamentally different frameworks of the cry may
be demonstrated by such decidedly "prophetic" uses of the cry as the following:
(a) the prophet Samuel uses the "royal" model of the cry to argue against the

selfsame model, citing the people's choosing of a king as the rationale for God's failure to answer their "cry" under domestic oppression, 1 Sam 8:18 (cf. similar prophetic uses of the "cry and no answer" pattern with regard to the worship of other gods—Jer 11:11, 12; Isa 57:13; Hos 7:14; cf. Judg 10:13, 14; and with regard to lack of justice—Mic 3:4; cf. Isa 5:7); (b) the repeated "revolutionary" use of "the cry of the marginal to the king" to set the actions of the king under the "judgment" of a prophet—1 Kgs 20:35-43 (for the king's failure to uphold the ban, v 42); 2 Kgs 6:26-31 (where the king reacts by swearing an oath to kill a prophet, v 31); and 2 Kgs 8:1-6 (where the king's judicial actions prove the wisdom of a prophet's previous advice, v 1); and (c) the actual usurping of the king's role as the hearer of the marginal's cry by the prophet himself, 2 Kgs 4:1-7, where Elisha hears the cry of a prophet's widow (*ṣā'ăqâ 'el-'elîšā'*, v 1) and responds to her statement of her case (*mah 'e'ĕśeh-lāk*, v 2), but here follows through not with a judicial decision, but with a miraculous intervention on her behalf (vv 2b-7).

There is thus a fundamental tension between the "royal" model of the marginal's cry to the king and the framework of the cry employed in the E traditions (and other literature with similar "prophetic" overtones) which is lacking in the framework shared by those materials similar to J. On the one hand, all that is needed to restore order in the J and similar materials is a judicial decision by the king, whether human or divine. On the other hand, in the E and similar materials, a more radical, often miraculous form of intervention is called for: slaves are not just to be treated fairly (Exod 5:15-18), but set free (Exod 3:10); oppressed nations are not just to be granted the rights of resident aliens (Exod 22:20), but themselves become the conquerors (Judg 3:10); widows do not just receive the property which is their right through legal appeal (2 Kgs 8:1-6), but they avoid the loss of children to slavery through the miraculous and over-abundant intervention of a prophet (2 Kgs 4:7). Thus while cues of syntax and situation argue that the cries in both these frameworks should be linked seman-tically to some degree with the cry of the marginal to the king, the manner in which God responds to this cry varies according to two patterns of intervention, here labeled "royal" (where the links between the cry of the marginal and this cry extend even through the "sentence") and "prophetic" (where the cry serves only as the grounds for another, more "revolutionary" pattern of "saving" which follows).

EXCURSUS—THE CRY AS A TECHNICAL TERM FOR PRAYER

As the object of the cry in the promise to Moses in both the J and E materials is restricted to God, it is only natural to question the overlap between this use of $z'q$ and $ṣ'q$ and that of *'tr*-qal and hif and *pll*-hitp, the subjects of a parallel excursus in Chapter 2. However, the consistency with which the former rather than the latter word-pair is chosen for this particular cry (both in the Exodus materials and the previously mentioned historical summaries) argues that, despite the shared object (i.e., God), these words should yet be distinguished according to the categories of process and action words versus words for brief, intense initiatory vocal activity. This is the case even though *'tr* and *pll* were seen, in a previous excursus, to occupy a more "intermediate" position between these two categories.

There are, however, other uses of $z'q$ and $s'q$ whose semantic parallels with *'tr* and *pll* are much closer. Several cues of syntax and situation point to the divergence between such uses of the "cry" and that found in the narratives of Exodus 3 and similar materials.

(1) *The use of variant prepositions.* In 1 Sam 7:9, the preposition *bĕ'ad* is used in conjunction with the verb $z'q$. Though this is the single occurrence of this preposition with this verb, it marks an "intercessory" use of the cry which is much more widespread. Beginning with the paired cries of the people and Moses at the sea (Exod 14:10, 15), several patterns of intercessory activity appear: (a) the community may "cry out" to Moses following which he intercedes on their behalf (e.g., Num 11:2); (b) the community may murmur against Moses following which he "cries out" to saving effect (e.g., Exod 15:25 and 17:4); and (c) an individual may request intercession following which Moses "cries out" on his or her behalf (e.g., Num 12:13). Such patterns of the intercessory cry continue through the DtrH (e.g., 1 Sam 7:8, 9; 2 Kgs 4:40 and 6:5 [though undirected, note the vocative]) to the later prophets. That this use of the cry overlaps that of *'tr* and *pll* can be seen both in those few places where they are used in parallel (e.g., Moses' intercessions on behalf of Pharaoh—Exod 8:8, 26; 10:18; cf. 9:33) and the numerous places where similar intercessory activity occurs using words syntagmatically similar to $z'q$ and $s'q$ (e.g., 1 Kgs 17:20, 21); "technical" terms for prayer, process, or action words (e.g., Num 21:7; 1 Sam 12:19, 23; 1 Kgs 13:6; 2 Kgs 4:33; Jer 15:11, 18:20, 37:3, 42:2-3); or both (e.g., Jer 7:16 and 11:14).

(2) *Inclusion of the notion of repentance.* There could not be a semantic dimension of the cry less probable with regard to the cries of the slaves in Egypt than that of penitence. As with the cry of the widow to the king, the "crime" in this situation is consistently that of another, be it a society's judicial procedures in general or as personified by the Pharaoh and his taskmasters. However, following the incident of the golden calf (Childs, *Exodus,* p. 258), a different pattern of the cry emerges. Here the necessity which provokes the cry is seen as arising not from a humanly inspired catastrophe, but from a divinely ordained punishment (e.g, Num 11:1-3). In this case, a penitential dimension of the cry is present which is given explicit content in such texts as Judg 10:10 and 1 Sam 12:10. Though such declaration of repentance may elsewhere be linked with the intercessory prayers described above (cf. 1 Sam 7:5-6), it must be noted that such penitential outcries are much less frequent than their intercessory counterparts and may be due more to later combinations of previously separate materials than any penitential aspect inherent to the vocalizations designated by $z'q$ or $s'q$ (note especially Brueggemann's argument where he identifies the first half of the Dtr formula—concerning Israel's rebellion and punishment, Judg 3:7-8; cf. 1 Sam 12:9—as a later addition to the earlier second half—which he categorizes as a

non-penitential cry for help followed by the saving acts of the deliverer; Brueggemann, "Social Criticism," pp. 101–114).

(3) *Switch from oppressed as subjects of the cry to various leaders who cry out on their behalf.* Regardless of the status of the above penitential cry, it and the intercessory cry share an essential formal characteristic which distinguishes both of them from the cry of the slaves in E. Instead of the initiatory cry of the person(s) in need playing the central role, there appears the cry of the leader acting on their behalf (cf. Exod 14:10, Num 11:2, and 2 Kgs 4:40, 6:5 with Exod 14:15, Num 12:13, and 1 Sam 7:8, 9).

It is this final observation which explains the placement of this excursus following the discussion of the framework of the cry in literary contexts similar to that of the E materials. Repeatedly, the leader who serves as the subject of such "technical" outcries is a "prophet," beginning as far back as the Elohist's story of Abraham and Abimelech in Genesis 20 (note v 7) and stretching through the prophets of the DtrH (Samuel, Elijah, Elisha) to the later prophets (Amos, Jeremiah, and Ezekiel). Though one should not make such an observation too axiomatic,[9] it is certainly tempting to list such uses of the cry *in these literary contexts*—E material in the Pentateuch, DtrH, and various places in the major and minor prophets—as another example of the way in which the "saving" function of the prophet is set over against that of the king.

In this regard, it is interesting to note the purpose clause in Israel's request for intercession to Samuel (1 Sam 7:8—"that he [God] might save us [wĕyōšiʿēnû] from the hands of the Philistines"; cf. the "resolution" of the Dtr formula in Judges, e.g. Judg 3:9) as well as a king's reaction to a similar request for intercession on another's behalf (2 Kgs 5:7; cf. v 11). Though, as with the use of the cry in general, other materials may place such intercessory functions under other titles (such as labeling the community laments in the Psalms as "royal" intercessions), within this group of material, this use of the cry as a technical term for prayer seems quite consistently linked with other forms of "saving" intervention here labeled "prophetic."

The Cry in Exod 6:2-8

And God said to Moses,
  "I am the Lord.
I appeared to Abraham, to Isaac, and to Jacob, as El Shaddai, but by my name YHWH I did not make myself known to them. Moreover, I estalished my covenant with them, to give them the land of Canaan, the land in which they lived as resident aliens. And now I myself have heard the moan of the Israelites whom the Egyptians have enslaved, and I have remembered my covenant.

---

[9] See Samuel E. Balentine, "The Prophet as Intercessor: A Reassessment," *Journal of Biblical Literature* 103 (1984) 161–73.

Say therefore to the Israelites,
'I am the Lord.
I will bring you out from under the burdens of the Egyptians, and I will deliver you
from their enslavement, and I will redeem you with an outstretched hand and with
great judgments. And I will take you for my people and I will be your God.

You will know that
I am the Lord
your God, who has brought you out from under the burdens of the Egyptians. I will
bring you into the land which I swore to give to Abraham, Isaac, and Jacob. I will
give it to you as a possession.

I am the Lord' "

(Exod 6:2-8)

The cry in the lamentation liturgy

If viewed solely within the context of the career of Moses, the words of
promise in Exod 6:2-8 might again be placed within a call narrative complete
with a commission (Exod 6:10-11 and 26-29), protest (Exod 6:12, 30), answer to
protest (Exod 6:13 and 7:1-5), and sign (Exod 7:8-13; see Plastaras, *Exodus,*
pp. 68-69 and Childs, *Exodus,* pp. 111-12). However, at the heart of this passage
stands *not* the pattern of "cry out and send" central to the cry in the E materials
above, but a pattern of "hearing" and remembering" (*šm'* and *zkr,* v 5) found
in neither the J nor the E version of the promise. Here the subjects of the finite
verbs describing the response to the cry are once again in the first person,
indicating God's return to center stage ("*I* have heard and remembered, therefore,
I will bring you out, deliver you, redeem you, etc."). The only finite verb of which
Israel is the subject is *yd',* "to know," in v 7, marking a contrast with the J
version in which it was God as judge who "knew" the condition of the slaves.
Most important, in the midst of such differences is the choice of a nominal form
of a word other than *z'q* or *s'q* to describe the slaves' vocalization. The word is
n'q, its nominal form *nĕ'āqâ,* here translated "the moan" of the Israelites. This
word's membership in chapter two's category of undirected and inarticulate cries
of pain ("Schmerzensschrei") may be demonstrated by its three non-
Pentateuchal occurrences in Judg 2:18 (a moan which moves God to pity), Ezek
30:24 (the moan of a "broken" king), and Job 24:12 (the moan of a city's dying
inhabitants).

How does one explain this shift in word choice in the promise within the
P materials? Several solutions are possible.

(1) *P's name schema.* One solution would be to link this shift to a cry of pain
with the progressive revelation of the names of God in the P material, repeated
in a summary form within Exod 6:2-8 itself (i.e., *'elōhîm* —v 2a, cf. Genesis 1,
'el-šaddāy —v 3, cf. Genesis 17; *yhwh*-vv 2, 3, 6, 7, 8, its first appearance in the
P materials). Unlike the nominal form of the cry in the J and E material (which
has been linked to its "judicial" function), the cry in the P material may be
undirected because the Israelites did not yet know *to whom,* specifically, they
should direct their cries (i.e., *yhwh*). Thus they simply "moaned" —undirected,

inarticulate. However, such a stress on this passage's discontinuity vis-a-vis the preceding P material (dividing history into the "moans" of pre-*yhwh* Israel and the "directed cries" of post-*yhwh* Israel) fails to recognize its own emphasis on its *continuity* vis-a-vis the same (particularly with regard to the "covenant" at the center of the following solution; cf. Childs, *Exodus,* pp. 113–14).

(2) *The covenant with the fathers.* The links of vocabulary and form between Exod 6:2–8 and Gen 17:1–8 are quite extensive.[10] Most important with regard to the use of the cry, however, is the focus of both passages on God's establishment of his covenant between himself and his people (*qôm*-hif plus *běrîtî,* Gen 17:7 and Exod 6:4). Not only does this "everlasting covenant" (*běrîtî ʿôlām,* Gen 17:7) prove the essential continuity between these two selections from the P material, it helps to explain their fundamental difference from the "see, hear, know, and come down" pattern of the promise in J and the "see and send" pattern in E. As God "sees" the rainbow in Gen 9:14–16 and thus "remembers" his covenant with all people, so he "hears" the moans of Israel in Exod 6:5 and thus "remembers" his special covenant with this particular people. However, even this shift fails to explain the use of *n'q* versus *z'q.* Could not God just as well "hear and remember" based on a directed cry for help as on an undirected cry of pain?

(3) *Setting within a lamentation liturgy.* Though several features of vocabulary (*šmʿ*—Exod 3:7 and 6:5; *šěpāṭîm gědōlîm*—Exod 6:6; cf. Exod 7:4; 12:12; Num 33:4; all P) and form (verification—Exod 6:5; sentence—Exod 6:6–8; cf. Plastaras, *Exodus,* pp. 71–72) argue for the continued "judicial" provenance of this version of God's promise to Moses, other features point toward a different life setting for this particular cry. Some features indicate a *general* "cultic" versus "judicial" setting for this "moan" on the part of Israel—such as the four-fold appearance of the "self-revelation formula," *ʾănî yhwh* (vv 2, 6, 7, and 8) and, more precisely, the measured nature of its repetition (exactly 23 words between the second and third, and the third and fourth occurrences), both of which point toward the identification of this passage as a "cultic formulary" (Plastaras, *Exodus,* pp. 72–74; cf. Childs, *Exodus,* p. 113). However, if one broadens the context and views this passage within the P materials in the first fifteen chapters of Exodus as a whole, a more particular setting within a liturgy of lamentation becomes possible—stretching from the "Lamentation" in Exod 2:23b–25 to the "Thanksgiving" in Exod 15:1–21. Within this variant life setting, this passage's specific function as a "Salvation-Oracle"[11] may be demonstrated by prophetic parallels with respect to vocabulary (e.g., *ydʿ,* "know"—Isa 41:20 and Exod 6:7; cf. Exod 6:3) and form ("assurance"—Isa 41:17 and Exod 6:5; "promise"—Isa

---

[10] See Norman C. Habel, *Literary Criticism of the Old Testament,* Guides to Biblical Scholarship, Old Testament Series (Philadelphia: Fortress Press, 1971), pp. 77–79.

[11] This term is here used to designate the form identified and described by J. Begrich, "Das priesterliche Heilsorakel," *Zeitschrift für alttestamentliche Wissenschaft* 52 (1934) 81–92.

41:8–19 and Exod 6:6–7a; and "purpose"—Isa 41:20 and Exod 6:7b; see Plastaras, *Exodus,* pp. 53–58).

This third solution to the choice of an undirected and inarticulate cry of pain for describing the vocalization of the slaves in Egypt is, finally, most convincing. Not only does it help explain the choice of a "moan" versus a cry "for help" (as the comparison with the vocabulary of similar literary contexts below will demonstrate), it helps to explain some of the features of the other two solutions as well: such as the "self-revelation formula" of the name schema (i.e., "cultic" provenance) and the centrality of the covenant in the covenantal solution (i.e., serves as the basis for such communal lamentations—see below). Needless to say, this change in life settings leads to some quite extensive differences in the conceptual framework of the cry.

The conceptual framework of the cry in the lamentation liturgy

In contrast to the uses of z^cq and $\d{s}^cq$ in the J and E versions of the promise—which were shown to be semantically similar to and functionally dissimilar from the cry of the marginal to the king—the use of $n^\prime q$ in the P version of the promise, while obviously dissimilar semantically, may be quite similar functionally, given the shift in life settings. Again, this contrast and comparison will be analyzed according to three complementary dimensions.

(1) *Implied cry for help.* There can be little doubt that, semantically, $n^\prime q$ and its nominal form represent an undirected, inarticulate cry of pain. As chapter two demonstrates, this variation in word choice from the use of nominal forms of z^cq and $\d{s}^cq$ in the J and E materials represents an essential shift. Gone is the intentionality, the hope for redress indicated by the "directing" of one's cry to another in the midst of necessity. However, one must leave open the possibility that in certain settings in life, even a cry of pain may *function* as a cry "for help." Though such a function seems improbable with respect to the "moaning" of a mortally wounded king (Ezek 30:24), it appears quite likely with respect to the "moaning" of the Israelites under oppression (Judg 2:18; cf. their "cry" in Judg 3:9) and the "moans" of a city's dying inhabitants (Job 24:12; cf. both the parallel verb, *šw* ', and the vocabulary of response, *śîm*). In a setting of communal lamentation, such a "for help" function becomes not only possible, but probable (as the narrative shift from the perfect tenses in relation to the moan, *šm* ' and *zkr,* to imperfect tenses in response to this moan, *ys*'-hif, *nṣl*-hif, etc., indicates). The shift from z^cq and $\d{s}^cq$ to $n^\prime q$ is thus quite significant for what it reveals concerning the *relationship* of "crier" and "hearer" within this particular framework of the cry. It is less significant with regard to how this vocalization *functions* in the narrative as a whole. In all three versions of the promise, it is the vocalization of the slaves, whether directed or undirected, which leads to God's "saving" response.

(2) *Special relationship.* The P version of the promise suffers from no dearth of proper names. God is identified by three names, the most "personal" of which, *yhwh,* is repeated four times within this passage. The "criers" in this account are

not nameless widows or the faceless victims of wicked cities, but the descendants of Abraham, Isaac, and Jacob (v 3). Here the designation "my people" is not forced into a framework with which it is at odds, but integrated structurally into a framework within which it is perhaps most at home ("and I will take you for my people and I will be your God," v 7; cf. Gen 17:8). Most important, at the center of this special relationship stands the "covenant," shifting the interaction between this people and God from that between a marginal and a righteous judge to that between covenant partners. While such characteristics as partiality and compassion would be inappropriate for the role of judge of all the earth, they are essential to the personal nature of Israel's and God's covenant. This people need not cry to God for justice (as a widow) or liberation (as a slave); all they need to do is "moan" and God will be moved to respond (as a parent to a child, or a friend to a friend). In this regard, note the difference in the mechanics of the cry between $z'q$ in Judg 3:9 and $n'q$ in Judg 2:18, where God responds because he "has compassion upon" (nhm-nif) the Israelites on account of their oppression.

(3) *Priestly remembrance of the covenant.* Repeatedly in the hymns of Israel, God is celebrated as a God who remembers his people![12] Again, such "memories" of past involvement would establish a conflict of interest in any life setting labeled "judicial." However, in the cult, and more important, in the liturgies of lamentation, such memories provide the grounds both for the people's undirected moaning and God's saving hearing. As the distinction between a directed cry "for help" and an undirected cry "of pain" marks a significant difference in the implied relation from which the people cry out, so the distinction between God's impartial investigation and his compassionate remembering marks a significant difference in the implied relation from which God hears this cry. Rather than the corresponding frameworks of the cry one might designate "royal" or "prophetic," this version of God's promise to Moses is set within one which might be labeled "priestly."

Other literary contexts which share this framework of the cry

An obvious move at this point would be to relate this framework of the cry to other literary contexts which revolve around similar cries of pain. One might analyze such contexts as the funeral lament of the individual (e.g., 2 Sam 19:5), the communal lament of Israel's enemies (e.g., Exod 11:6 and 12:30; 1 Sam 5:10; cf. that of Israel in 1 Sam 4:13-14), and such special uses of the lamentation theme as the summons to communal lamentation (imperative forms mentioned at beginning of chapter 3) or the ambiguous prophetic "outcries" of Hab 1:2 (an individual lament adapted to a communal function?) or Jer 20:8 (a prophetic announcement of coming destruction?).

---

[12] See Brevard S. Childs, *Memory and Tradition in Israel,* Studies in Biblical Theology (London: SCM Press, 1962) p. 44.

However, the key to this particular framework of the cry is the special relationship at its core and the pattern of "cry out and remember" which reflects this. Therefore, one should not expect a similar use of the cry except in literary contexts which share all these features, namely liturgies of lamentation on the part of Israel itself. One such literary context, the book of Lamentations, has here been chosen as exemplary.

First of all, one might note that the preponderance of undirected cries "of pain" versus directed cries "for help" is here obvious from the first chapter on. In chapter one, Zion is depicted as a widow in mourning (1:1–2). Though her "marginal" status might entitle her to appeal to Yahweh as judge to hear her case, she does not. Instead, "she" — as embodied in the roads to Zion (1:4), a despoiled Jerusalem (1:8), all her people (1:1), and herself in the first person (1:21) — "groans" ($'nh$) with her face turned away (1:8). In this setting of lamentation, the only form of $z'q$ or $s'q$ (besides the imperative form in 2:18, see Wolff, "Aufruf") is absolute and without explicit content (3:8; cf. Hab 1:2; Job 19:7; Jer 20:8). Undirected and inarticulate, Jerusalem's vocalizations register only pain.

Nevertheless, parallel terms indicate that, *in this setting,* even such "Schmerzensschrei" may function as cries for help. Two times in Lamentations the "Hilferuf," $\check{s}w'$, occurs — once in parallel with the absolute use of $z'q$ (3:8), once in a petition to God not to close his ears (3:56). Because of who Zion is and who the Lord is in relation to her, even her groans may *function* as cries for help.

Further, the special relationship within which these cries of pain occur is identified by the use of the theme of remembrance central to the P framework of the cry. God is called not only to "see" Zion's affliction ($r'h$, 1:9, 11, 12, 20, etc.) and to "hear" how she groans ($\check{s}m'$, 1:21), but he is summoned pre-eminently to "remember" Zion's afflictions (zkr, 3:19 and 5:1) and thus, by implication, the past glories which the widowed Jerusalem now so painfully recalls (zkr, 1:7). Such a call to remembrance is not the language one directs toward a judge in a legal proceeding, but the pain one voices in the presence of one with whom one once shared a relationship characterized by such terms as "loyalty" (*hesed*) and "compassion" (*rahămîm*, 3:22), but who now not only fails to "remember" (zkr, 2:1) but seems purposefully to forget (*škḥ*-pi, 5:20). On the basis of this special relationship, the speaker of Lamentations summons Jerusalem to a communal lamentation (2:18–19) in hopes that God will once again "hear and remember" as he did once long ago in Egypt (Exod 6:5).

II. THE INTRODUCTORY CRY IN EXOD 2:23b–25

And the people of Israel groaned from enslavement, and cried out, and their cry for help from enslavement came up to God. God heard their moan and God remembered his covenant with Abraham and Isaac and Jacob. God saw the people of Israel and God knew [their plight] (Exod 2:23b–25).

In one sense, the first canonical reference to the cry of the slaves serves as the perfect introduction to the P version of the promise in Exod 6:2-8. Here is the P framework of the cry in outline—the vocabulary of lament ('*nḥ*, v 23, cf. Lam 1:9, 11, etc.; *z'q*—absolute, v 23, cf. Lam 3:8; *šw'*, v 23, cf. Lam 3:8, 56) located in the context of a special relationship (note the seven-fold repetition of the major actors—two times, *běnê-yiśrā'ēl;* five times, *'ĕlōhîm*) characterized particularly by God's "hearing" of this people's "moan" (*wayyišma' 'ĕlōhîm 'et-na'ăqātām*) and his "remembering" of his covenant with Abraham, Isaac, and Jacob (*wayyizkōr 'ĕlōhîm 'et-běrîtô 'et-'abrāhām 'et-yiṣḥāq wě'et-ya'ăqōb,* cf. Exod 6:5). There can be little doubt that this "priestly" framework of the cry is attributable to this cry's location in a setting of communal lamentation. Indeed, as mentioned above, this passage quite likely functions as the introductory "lamentation" preceding the "oracle of salvation" in Exodus 6 and the "thanksgiving" in Exodus 15. Together, they constitute a full-fledged liturgy of lamentation which provides the structural outline of the first fifteen chapters of Exodus as finally redacted by the P school (see again, Plastaras, *Exodus,* pp. 49–59).

Even so, it is in this broader sense—as an introduction to the structural outline of the opening chapters of Exodus *as a whole*—that this first canonical reference to the cry must be seen as an introduction to the J and E versions of the promise *in particular*. It is in this respect that Exod 2:23b-25 goes beyond Exod 6:2-8 with regard both to what precedes and to what follows its central pattern of God's "hearing and remembering."

Before

As demonstrated above, placing the vocabulary of the "Schmerzensschrei" within a setting of communal lamentation may allow such cries "of pain" to function as cries "for help." However, here the "for help" tendencies of this cry are not merely implied by such a setting in life. In this passage, three words for vocalization occur in a sequence which moves through the word field of the "cry" from an unambiguous cry of pain ('*nḥ*); to a borderline cry of pain or cry for help (*z'q*); to a usually quite unambiguous cry for help (*šw'*). Furthermore, this "progression" ends with the "going up" of a nominal form of the cry to God ('*lh*-hif with a nominal form of *šw'*). The movement indicated between these verbs argues that this final cry has shifted away from the identical cry of the defeated city in 1 Sam 5:12 toward the evidential cry in Exod 3:9 which "comes up" to God the judge. The P version of the cry seems here to anticipate the E version of the cry which follows.

After

The long list of first person verbs with God as subject is shared by this passage with its counterpart in Exodus 6. Furthermore, though only God's "hearing" is present in Exodus 6, the above study of Lamentations demonstrates that his "seeing" of oppression may be a common theme in such settings of communal lamentation. However, this series of first person verbs ends with an awkward use of the verb *yd'* without an object, a verb which in Exodus 6 has the people, not God, as subject. This final first person verb argues for a possible tension in the settinq of this series of verbs which points toward God's judicial "seeing, hearing, and knowing" in Exod 3:7. The P version of the cry seems here to anticipate the J version which follows.

There is thus a sense in which this first canonical reference to the cry of the slaves serves as a proper introduction to the multi-faceted uses of the cry in the J and E material and, through the conceptual frameworks established on the basis of their analysis, to the multifaceted uses of the cry in the canon as a whole. Though Exod 2:23b-25's overall "framing" function sets all the cries of Exodus 1-15 finally within a setting of communal lamentation, it does so without erasing the diversity of settings and conceptual frameworks which lie behind these various versions of the cry. It is, finally, the canonical mixture of such varying vocabularies, settings, and frameworks of human vocalizations which reveals the rich semantic possibilities tapped by the Old Testament's varied uses of the words *z'q* and *s'q* and the associated words of their field.

EXCURSUS—THE CRY IN THE PSALTER

In one sense, this mixture of unity and diversity in the biblical use of the cry is demonstrated nowhere quite as well as in the Psalms. Here all three of the above-mentioned frameworks of the cry are evident: (1) *the royal pattern*—where the portrait of both the earthly and the heavenly king as legal protector of the marginal (Ps 72:1-4, 12-14; 146:7-9) is fleshed out in terms of the latter's particular attention to the "cries of the oppressed" (*sa'āqat 'ănāyîm*, Ps 9:13); (2) *the prophetic pattern*—where the central pattern of "cry out/send" is occasionally present (*z'q/slh*, Ps 107:19, 20); and (3) *the priestly pattern*—where the shift from directed cries for help (e.g., Ps 77:2, *wě'es'āqâ*) to undirected cries of pain (e.g., Ps 77:4, *wě'ehěmāyâ*) is evident.

However, in another sense, this diversity may be more apparent than real. First of all—given the centrality of this cry in the preceding biblical narratives of the Exodus and the comprehensive nature of the Psalter—the occurrences of *z'q* and *s'q* in the Psalms are extremely limited (only 11 occurrences out of the host of "cries, groans, etc." in the Psalms). Second, even though a diversity of conceptual frameworks seems to be employed, these frameworks often demonstrate significant shifts away from those patterns revealed in the narrative sections of the Old Testament (note the shift from the "marginal" to the "righteous" [*saddîqîm*] in Ps 34:18 [see *LXX;* correct in sense—cf. v 16—if not in meter], and the "sending" not of a saving prophet but God's saving "word" [*děbārô*] in Ps 107:20). Third, and most important, the remaining uses of the cry demonstrate a strong preference for only one of these frameworks, the priestly, a point which might be demonstrated both by looking at the occurrences of *z'q* and *s'q* as a whole (i.e., the repeated use of *z'q* and *s'q* as lead words in laments of the individual, Ps 79:2; 88:2; 142:2, 6) and by examining the movement of thought in one of the Psalms of which one of these words is a part (e.g., Psalm 77 — note the underlying framework of "cry out/remember" [v 2/vv 4, 12; cf. v 10], underlining God's "special" versus "impartial" relationship with this people of which the crier is a member [e.g., vv 8-10, 16, 21 — note the emphasis on promises, compassion, and proper names]).

All of this leads one to conclude that whatever the life setting of the Psalms (a field of research into which this excursus chooses not to enter), it was one which proved fairly incompatible with the general thought world associated with z^cq and s^cq. In the Psalms, as in the Priestly version of the Exodus cry, cries of pain uttered within the context of a special covenantal relationship predominate. Here cries functioning within processes which presume no such special relationship are only "looked back on" as being appropriate for the "fathers" (e.g., Ps 22:6) or representative of the covenant community as a whole (e.g., Ps 107:6, 13, 19, 28; cf. the fixed form of these cries in the past with the previously mentioned historical summaries of Num 20:16; Deut 26:7; Josh 24:7; etc.). However, when the individual in the Psalms cries out, whatever the identity of that individual might be (another field of research not to be broached), he or she voices not pre-eminently a cry for justice or liberation. Rather, this individual utters a cry of pain within the context of precedents and promises which argue that such heart-felt "Schmerzensschreie," when voiced by members of this covenant community, do not, or should not go unheard.

III. CONCLUSIONS

In various ways, this chapter illustrates the power conveyed by the placement of words within the third and final context of literary setting. Chapter 2 attempted to demonstrate the power of communication inherent in the choice of one word rather than another within its field. The results there were illuminating, but limited, focusing primarily on the unique capacity of z^cq and s^cq to capture the subtle semantic nuances separating an undirected cry of pain from a directed cry for help. Chapter 3 attempted to demonstrate the power of communication achieved by relocating a word within a particular social setting especially significant for its use within the language world of which it is a part. There the results were slightly more dramatic, enabling one to supply categories for the "crier" and the "cried to" and the nature of the interaction between the two.

It is, however, the final move, the location of these words within their literary settings in the scriptures, which ultimately proves most significant. Here, for the first time, the *particular* aspects of these words' meaning intended by those who employed them become apparent. What is most striking at this point is that those particularities of meaning differ, leading to a variety of conceptual frameworks of the cry and even to variant choices of words. At the very beginning of the Exodus narratives in the canon of Old Testament Scriptures, a rich diversity of thought emerges as to the identity of those who cry out and the one they cry to, the nature of the process they intend to provoke, and the reasons why this process moves forward: a divine judge comes down to judge and save on the basis of an appeal by the legally marginal; a prophetic liberator is sent forth to deliver one national group from another on the basis of the protesting outcry of the oppressed; a covenant partner is moved to remember on the basis of the pain-filled moans of the worshiping community upon whom he has especially placed his promises.

Here the more abstract discussions of word-choice and social setting take on both power and significance. It is the significance of these now uncovered patterns of appropriation of the slaves' cry which will serve as the heart of the discussion in the following, concluding chapter.

5
Conclusions

Theologically, it was always extraordinarily significant for Israel
that its beginnings as a people were grounded in a cry for help.

Hasel, *TDOT* 4:120

Given the widespread occurrence of the basic pattern of "cry out/save" in the most diverse Old Testament materials and particularly the fixity of the "cry" portion of this pattern when used as a refrain for looking back to the cries of the fathers in the past (see introduction), an *early* formulation of this basic assertion of Israel seems quite likely, whatever may be the date of the later accretions which gathered around it or the later modifications which may have evolved from it (see again references at beginning of chapter 3 to scholars who argue against von Rad's *early* dating of the little "credo" often on the basis of the "lateness" of some of its constituent parts). However, this dissertation has not been an attempt to trace the "growth" of the biblical idea of the cry; rather it has been an attempt to analyze the use of the cry as given by the biblical texts themselves, from the vantage point of the various contexts of vocabulary, situation, and literature. It remains to draw out some of the implications of the usage of z^cq and s^cq thereby revealed. This will be attempted in three sections: the first of which will use the findings of chapters 2 and 3 to discuss the significance of the Old Testament's choice of these words for vocalizations directed toward God; the second of which will use the findings of chapter 4 to discuss the biblical appropriation of the cry; and the third of which will ask what such findings may have to say about the patterns of such cries in God's future, particularly as it is revealed to Christians in the life, death, and resurrection of Jesus Christ.

I. THE SIGNIFICANCE OF THE CHOICE OF Z^cQ/S^cQ FOR VOCALIZATIONS DIRECTED TOWARD GOD

If one defines "prayer" simply as any vocalization directed toward God (versus the more precise definitions of technical terms for "prayer" in the preceding excurses), one must not underestimate the significance of the repeated selection of z^cq and s^cq to express one of the fundamental patterns of prayer in the Old Testament, beginning with the "prayer" of the slaves in Egypt. The choice of these words signaling a brief, intense, and initiatory cry for help whose function is dramatically embodied in the cry of the marginal to the king for legal hearing has implications for any theology of Old Testament prayer in general and for many of the current trends in the theology of prayer in particular.

Perhaps most important in this regard is the previously mentioned capacity of these two words to capture the subtle semantic differences between an undirected and therefore isolated cry "of pain" and a directed and therefore non-isolated cry "for help." This difference between an animal-like groan and an inter-human appeal for help is central to defining any situation of interaction which might be designated "petitionary." As Erhard Gerstenberger states regarding the necessary prologue for any interpersonal "Bittsituation," or act of petition, "Every person becomes a petitioner whenever he cannot overcome a problem alone and seeks refuge or help from his fellow human beings" (Gerstenberger, *Der bittende Mensch,* p. 17). The various cues marking the slight, but nevertheless extremely significant differences in meaning between $z'q$ and $s'q$ as a "Schmerzensschrei" and these same two words as a "Hilferuf" enable one to capture in a unique way this initial turning to seek help from another.

The second step of our argument has centered on the recognition that what is true of inter-human speech is also true of biblical speech between persons and God. Here our primary concern has again been that of the "Bittsituation"; this time, however, those particular acts of petition we label "prayer." As Moshe Greenberg states, "[the] patterns [of prose prayers in the Bible] are similar to the representation of interhuman speech patterns in analogous circumstances" (Greenberg, *Biblical Prose Prayer,* p. 35). By this move, the biblical use of $z'q$ and $s'q$ becomes revelatory not only for fleshing out the "situation of need," the "relationship of the participants," and the "actual characteristics of the request" in acts of petition *between people* (i.e., a marginal and the king), but for similar interactions *between people and God.* Thus the root $z'q/s'q$ becomes "an important component of the biblical motif of solidarity, which binds human beings together as a group as well as binding them to God" (Hasel, *TDOT* 4:116).

It is thus all the more striking how the *petitionary* thrust of such fundamental Old Testament "prayers" as the cry of the slaves in Egypt is missed or rejected by most modern theologies of prayer. Here the anti-petitionary stance of both scholarly and popular works on prayer (see introduction) must be contrasted with the following selections from Karl Barth's Dogmatics on the subject of prayer! *If* the above analyses of $z'q$ and $s'q$ are anywhere close to the mark, and *if* one accepts the assumption that their widespread use testifies to their fundamental importance for any Old Testament theology of prayer, there can be little doubt as to who is closest to the mark in biblical terms.

On the petitionary heart of true prayer (cf. the "Hilferuf," chapter 2):

> Prayer is decisively petition—petition addressed to God (3/4:97).

---

[1] Karl Barth, *Church Dogmatics,* edited by G. W. Bromiley and T. F. Torrance, vol. 3/3, 4: *The Doctrine of Creation* (Edinburgh: T. & T. Clark, 1960–61).

On the approach of the "crier" to the "cried to" (cf. the "situation of need," chapter 3):

> In the first instance, it [prayer] is an asking, a seeking and a knocking directed towards God; a wishing, a desiring and a requesting presented to God . . . The man who really prays comes to God and approaches and speaks to Him because he seeks something of God, because he desires and expects something, because he hopes to receive something he needs, something which he does not hope to receive from anyone else but does definitely hope to receive from God (3/3:268).

On the brevity of such outcries (cf. the "content of the vocalization," chapter 2):

> A request, or even a series of requests, is soon uttered if it is close to our hearts. Hence true prayer may and must probably be short rather than long (3/4:112).

On the tendency toward inarticulateness of true prayer (cf. the "content of the vocalization," chapter 2):

> The distinctive feature of the specific, conscious, and express prayer required by the divine commandment is that like confession it takes the form of speech . . . [However] even in common prayer it not only can but must and will be decisively an inward speaking, which in its inadequacy as human speaking to this Other, and in consciousness of this inadequacy, will be simply a sighing and stammering, both in its beginning and in its end (3/4:89).

On the radical disparity between the "crier" and the "cried to" which serves not as an obstacle to, but as the very basis for prayer (cf. the identity of the participants, chapter 3):

> When he comes to God simply with his request, he comes with empty hands. But empty hands are necessary when human hands are to be spread out before God and filled by Him. It is these empty hands that God in His goodness wills of us when He bids us pray to Him. He who is obedient to Him is ready to begin at the beginning every time he prays. He always understands God as the unique source of all good and himself as absolutely needy in relation to Him. He puts himself joyfully under this fundamental law of the covenant relationship. He has nothing either to represent or to present to God except himself as the one who has to receive all things from Him (3/4:97).

II. THE BIBLICAL APPROPRIATION OF THE EXODUS CRY

The writers, editors, and compilers of the various traditions in the Exodus material were not slaves in the Egypt of the Pharaohs. Thus they could not "cry out" within the identical convergent contexts from which their enslaved ancestors did. Necessarily, they set about the process of somehow "appropriating" this cry for themselves using language, situations, and literary contexts intelligible to the people of their day. As the three complementary analyses in chapter four indicate, different writers, editors, and compilers went about this "appropriation" in different ways. The following is an attempt to link the varying frameworks within which the various traditions placed this cry with the particular socio-historical settings from which these various traditions arose.

The "Royal" Appropriation of the Cry by the J Traditions

As the comparative analysis of the stories of Cain and Abel and Sodom and Gomorrah indicates, the J traditions, more so than either of the others, adopted the royal, judicial setting of the marginal's cry to the king as that life setting most appropriate for interpreting the semantics and the function of the cry of the slaves in Egypt to God. Though the shift to nominal forms of the cry indicated a slight shift in the precise scene (from the initial cry of the marginal to the king's prosecution of a case on the basis of this cry), the J traditions accepted without question the essential validity of setting the cry within a framework whose order was preserved by the legal actions of a royal judge.

This should not be surprising given the probable compilation of the J traditions during the "golden days" of Israel's monarchy.[2] Here the life setting of the marginal's appeal to the king would be readily accessible to the hearers of the stories preserved by the Yahwist. It was undoubtedly by means of just such stories of the royal preservation of order through the king's hearing of the cries of widows, orphans, and resident aliens that the people heard the monarchs of their day praised. It was thus a short step from this human portrait of order to that maintained by the royal judge in heaven.

It must be noted here, however, that while such a framework made the cry of the slaves as recalled by the J traditions easily intelligible, it did not make this *cry for justice* easy to appropriate by *all* those who heard it so recounted. Here the categories of the relationship between the "criers" and the "cried to" were kept quite precise *legally.* Though *all* the people in tenth century Israel *had been* "strangers" in Egypt via their enslaved ancestors, they were not all such legal marginals *now.* Therefore, this particlar version of the slaves' cry most likely functioned quite similarly to its counterpart in the Covenant Code (Exod 22:21-23), reminding the people of Israel of their origins so that they might be cognizant of the marginals in their midst. Thereby they might continue to claim the part of the slaves whose cry was heard by God in the Exodus narrative rather than the part of Pharaoh and his taskmasters whose cries at the sea were not (cf. Prov 21:13).

The "Prophetic" Appropriation of the Cry by the E Traditions

Other writers, compilers, and editors of the biblical materials undoubtedly found the "royal" framework of the cry an appropriate model for understanding God's response to the various cries for help in his world (as the preceding study

---

[2] See n. 4 in chapter 4.

of Job's use of this framework to bring God to trial indicates). However, such a framework of the cry would be particularly inappropriate for writers, editors, and compilers during a time when the earthly model of the king's preservation of order had failed or was failing and the cries of society's marginals for legal hearing were going unheard.

Several scholars have proposed just such a socio-historical setting for the compilation of the E traditions.[3] In the North, sometime between the establishment and the fall of the Northern Kingdom, various scattered circles set about the preservation of a set of traditions often at odds with the more "royally" inclined traditions of the South. Variously described as the *'am hā'āres*; prophetic circles; or "rural, popular elements"; these circles often saw the model of a royal preservation of order not as a solution, but as the heart of the problem itself.

If such social categories have any validity at all, the particular appropriation of the cry by the E traditions becomes easily intelligible. Though yet sharing in the semantics of the marginal's appeal to the king, the actual method of intervention here differs radically. From a preservation of the status quo through royal judicial proceedings, one moves toward the disruption and overthrow of such order through the miraculous intervention of "saviors" in opposition to earthly kings, both foreign and domestic. This *cry for liberation* thus could be appropriated by any and all who saw themselves as sharing this "over against" stance; any who in many and various ways saw themselves as oppressed by the societies in which they lived. Such people, like the slaves in Egypt, could cry out to God in hope that even now he would send a liberator who would save them from the political oppression which they shared.

The "Priestly" Appropriation of the Cry by the P Traditions

The experience of the exile was undoubtedly a seminal event in the history of Israel. None of Israel's previous constructs could survive the experience of the destruction of God's temple and the deportation of his people without undergoing at least some shifts in emphases, if not radical reversals in underlying assumptions. Surely at the center of such theological paradigm shifts was the shape of those traditions connected with Israel's beginning exile in and exodus from Egypt.

One need not date all the traditions contained in the P materials exilic or post-exilic in order to identify their final compilation as such. Likewise, one does not have to prove the liturgy of communal lamentation exilic or post-exilic in order to posit such a date for the P school's elevation of this liturgy to a place of central importance. Where else but the exile would such a shift from judicial

[3] For an example, see Alan W. Jenks, *The Elohist and North Israelite Traditions,* Society of Biblical Literature Monograph Series, no. 22 (Missoula: Scholars Press, 1977) pp. 101–6. Further bibliography is provided by T. E. Fretheim, "Elohist," *Interpreter's Dictionary of the Bible, Supplementary Volume* (Nashville: Abingdon, 1976) p. 263.

cries for justice and political cries for liberation to cultic *cries of pain* in the context of remembered covenantal promises be both more easily explicable or more necessary (cf. previous citations from Lamentations)?

Nevertheless, the shift in life settings necessary for this priestly appropriation of the cry of the slaves in Egypt brought with it some quite radical shifts in the particular group of people who could now claim this Exodus cry as their own. On the one hand, this group was drastically broadened, leaving behind the J and E frameworks of the cry which restricted those who might cry out according to either legal or political categories. On the other hand, this group was drastically narrowed, through the adoption of a cultic framework of the cry grounded in the special relationship between God and his covenant people. As the categories of the "poor and needy" broaden and narrow in the Psalms according to the various contexts in which they are understood, so the cry of the slaves is here both broadened in a socio-political sense and narrowed in a religiospiritual sense by placing this cry on the lips of any member of the covenant community who cries out in pain within a liturgy of communal lamentation.

This study of the biblical appropriation of the Exodus cry thus guards against any one-dimensional approach to the significance of this cry of the slaves for the faith and worship of Israel. Central to this cry's far-reaching importance for the biblical traditions as a whole is its ability to be heard and appropriated by different people in different ways at different times. Perhaps contrary to first impressions, the extensive adaptability of this Exodus cry is due less to a general lack of precision in the particular words chosen to express this vocalization than to these words' ability to signify a variety of quite specific meanings according to the overall conceptual framework within which they are placed.

Finally, it is this combination of specificity and adaptability which has the most to say to present-day uses of the slaves' cry, as in the various theologies of liberation mentioned in the introduction. The foregoing study of the various patterns of appropriation by the writers, editors, and compilers of the Old Testament both buttresses and challenges such modern "applications" of the cry.

On the one hand, the particularity of these patterns of appropriation drives home the correctness of a concrete location of the cry within the pains and injustices of one's own socio-historical setting. As in the *J traditions,* the cry may be located in the appeals of the legally marginal for justice, a cry to which God as judge of all the earth is especially obligated to respond, both with salvation for those who cry out and judgment against those who have caused or failed to hear such cries (Exod 3:7-8; cf. Exod 22:20-23 and Prov 21:13). As in the *E traditions,* the cry may be located in the pleas of various national groups for liberation, a cry which leads to God's raising up of "prophetic" liberators to challenge the excesses of "royal" structures, but also a cry whose answering may sometimes presage the chasing after other gods and the necessary entry of a penitential dimension of the cry (Exod 3:9-10; cf. Judg 10:10-16). As in the *P traditions,* the cry may be located in the pain-filled cries of the covenant community in worship, a cry which causes God to remember the unique nature of his relationship with this special people due to promises made long ago (Exod 6:2–8; cf. selections from Lamentations). The Old Testament does not shy away from giving recognizable faces to those who cry out by locating those cries through the use of particular language, from particular social situations, placed within particular literary settings.

On the other hand, the wide-ranging nature of these patterns of appropriation cautions against any final restriction of this slaves' cry's adaptability. Perhaps what rings most true to the biblical use of the cry is the challenge to hear this cry in continually new and various ways; to hold on to the particularity that this cry so dramatically represents, but not to limit such particularity to any single social or political or liturgical category. That the adaptability of this cry may ultimately be even more authoritative than its ingrained particularity becomes especially obvious as one shifts from past patterns of appropriation to the patterns of the cry in God's future.

III. PATTERNS OF THE CRY IN THE FUTURE

If the cry of humanity to God has revealed patterns of thought and hope fundamental to the faith and worship of the Old Testament, it would be highly unusual if these patterns of the cry were not also employed to describe God's continued involvement with his world in the future. Though a detailed analysis of such patterns of language and thought beyond the Old Testament would entail another series of analyses altogether (such as a study of the word field, settings in life, and settings in literature of the cry in the New Testament), a more limited indication of the possibilities of such an approach might be demonstrated by a passing glance at several descriptions of the cry in God's future by the prophet Isaiah. For purposes of continuity, these "patterns" of the cry will be listed according to the three primary "frameworks" of the cry discussed above.

"Royal" Framework of the Cry

As the Yahwist depicted a time in distant history when God the divine king came down to act as judge on behalf of the marginals who cried out to him for legal hearing, so Israel dreamed of a future human king who, as God's special representative, would establish such a just rule on earth. This king's legal capabilities would not be limited to evidence accessible to the judicial "seeing" and "hearing" of the past (Isa 11:36), but with "righteousness" he would judge the poor, and with "equity" decide for the afflicted of the earth (Isa 11:4a). Moreover, this king's throne would be established forever (Isa 9:7); this king would never cry out the absolute cry of the vanquished (Isa 42:2).[4] This king would not fail until he had established justice on a universal scale (Isa 42:4). As such just rules of the king in the past were embodied by narratives of the king

---

[4] See Ralph Marcus, "The 'Plain Meaning' of Isaiah 42:1–4," *The Harvard Theological Review* 30 (1937) 259. Compare the cry of other "shepherds," e.g. Jer. 25:36.

responding to the marginals' cries, so the writers of the New Testament may well declare the inauguration of just such an eternal rule in their stories of a "king" from Nazareth who turns repeatedly during his earthly ministry to hear the cries of the oppressed (cf. the form of Mark's story of the healing of blind Bartimaeus, Mark 10:46–52: Jesus' passing by, Bartimaeus' crying out, Jesus' turning and inquiry, Bartimaeus' request, and Jesus' imperative "judgment" of healing; cf. 1 Kgs 20:35–43).

"Prophetic" Framework of the Cry

As noted, one characteristic of the E framework of the cry was the sending of a savior to deliver one people with a name from another people with a name. From the cry of the slaves through Judges and the DtrH, the particular people to be delivered were quite consistently the people of Israel (*běnê-yiśrā'ēl*, e.g. Exod 3:16; Judg 3:9; etc.). The exclusive nature of this group of the "oppressed" was undoubtedly linked to the entire "over against" social context from which this framework of the cry arose (see above). With Isaiah, however, the possibility emerges that other national groups might be included in the characteristically "particular" group of those who cry out under oppression. Here, according to Isaiah, not just any national group, but those original oppressors of the Israelites, the Egyptians, will cry out to God on account of their oppressors (*yiṣ'ăqû 'el-yhwh mippěnê lōḥăsîm*) and God will send a savior (*wěyišlaḥ lāhem môšîa'*) to defend and deliver them (Isa 19:20). Again, the writers of the New Testament describe the sending of another "savior" to deliver Gentile as well as Jew so that the author of Romans may subsequently proclaim: "everyone who calls upon the Lord will be saved" (Rom 10:13; cf. Joel 3:5, *kōl 'ăšer-yiqrā' běšēm yhwh yimmālēṭ*).

"Priestly" Framework of the Cry

However, if the "royal" and "prophetic" frameworks of the cry prove amenable to such broadened categories as Isaiah looks toward the future, the "priestly" framework does not. With regard to God's hearing and remembering in response to this cry of pain on the part of his covenant people, the distinction between those who are *within* and those *without* the relationship fundamental to this pattern of the cry only increases. On the one hand, the sound of Zion's outcry (*lěqôl za'ăqekā*) will continue to be heard and answered (Isa 30:19b). Indeed, before the people of Jerusalem call out (*wěhāyâ ṭerem-yiqrā'û*), they will be answered (Isa 65:24), so that, eventually, no more shall be heard in this city the sound of weeping (*qôl běkî*) or the communal outcry of distress (*wěqôl zě'āqâ*, Isa 65:19). On the other hand, the subsequent shouts of God's servants due to gladness of heart (*yārōnnû miṭṭûb lēb*) must be contrasted with the continued crying out of their enemies due to pain of heart (*tiṣ'ăqû mikkě'ēb lēb*) and their communal wailing due to anguish of spirit (*ûmiššēber rûaḥ těyēlîlû*, Isa 65:14).

One can only wonder at this point how the placement of a similar "Schmerzensschrei" on the lips of a "king" on a cross by the writers of the New Testament passion accounts affects Isaiah's radical dichotomy with respect to this pattern of the cry. In one sense, the apparent non-hearing of this cry of pain on the part of one whose claims regarding a special relationship with God were the cause of his death seems to deny Isaiah's vision of a future when God's people's cries would not go unanswered, even momentarily. In another sense, as this cry is recalled from the perspective of God's saving answer in the resurrection, it may well mark only the end of the cry as heard and remembered within one covenant and the beginning of a new age of the cry within another. It is within the framework of this new covenant that the people of the new Israel, Christ's church, are able to reclaim and reappropriate that fundamental profession of the Old Testament:

> "Then we cried to the Lord the God of our fathers,
> and the Lord heard our voice and . . ."

Appendixes

Though the materials in these appendixes are not integral to the comprehension of the text, they may well provide a means of looking back over the dissertation as a whole. Presented as handouts at a colloquy near the end of this paper's formulation, they consist of: (1) a chart representing the development of the argument in capsule form; (2) a summary of the conceptual frameworks of the cry at the heart of chapter four; and (3) a question regarding the significance of the patterns of the biblical appropriation of the cry for similar attempts at appropriation today.

APPENDIX A

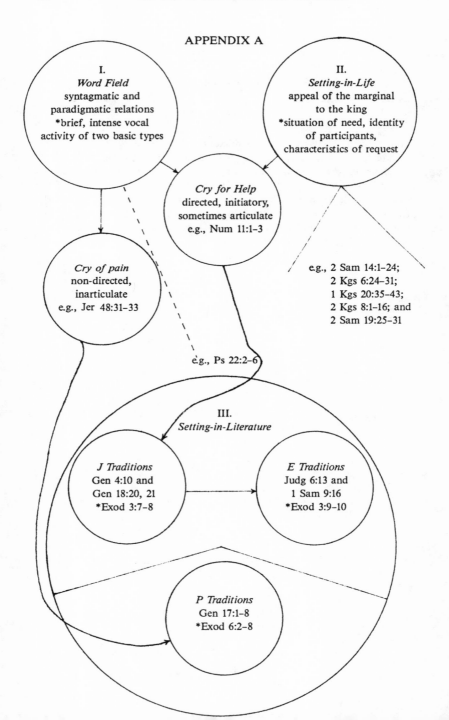

I.
Word Field
syntagmatic and
paradigmatic relations
*brief, intense vocal
activity of two basic types

II.
Setting-in-Life
appeal of the marginal
to the king
*situation of need, identity
of participants,
characteristics of request

Cry for Help
directed, initiatory,
sometimes articulate
e.g., Num 11:1–3

Cry of pain
non-directed,
inarticulate
e.g., Jer 48:31–33

e.g., 2 Sam 14:1–24;
2 Kgs 6:24–31;
1 Kgs 20:35–43;
2 Kgs 8:1–16; and
2 Sam 19:25–31

e.g., Ps 22:2–6

III.
Setting-in-Literature

J Traditions
Gen 4:10 and
Gen 18:20, 21
*Exod 3:7–8

E Traditions
Judg 6:13 and
1 Sam 9:16
*Exod 3:9–10

P Traditions
Gen 17:1–8
*Exod 6:2–8

APPENDIX B

CONCEPTUAL FRAMEWORKS FOR THE APPROPRIATION OF THE SLAVES' CRY

A. *Within God's Words of Promise to Moses*
  (1) as preserved in the *J Traditions* (a socio-legal approach)
       — a cry "against," nominal forms of the cry
       — no special relationship, marginal/king
       — "royal" preservation of order
    cf. framework of cry in Job (e.g., Job 19:7)
  (2) as preserved in the *E Traditions* (a socio-political approach)
       — the cry as summons or grounds for a call, cry out/send
       — participants particularized/nationalized
       — "prophetic" disruption of order
    cf. framework of cry in DtrH (e.g., Judg 3:10)
  (3) as preserved in the *P traditions* (a liturgical approach)
       — cry of pain, *n'q*
       — special relationship
       — "priestly" remembrance of the covenant
    cf. framework of cry in Lamentations (e.g., Lam 3:8)

B. *Within the Introductory Cry of Exod 2:23b–25*
  (1) centered on P's framework of "hear/remember"
    "God heard their moaning and God remembered his covenant"
  (2) anticipates E's framework, the "coming up" of the cry
    "the people of Israel groaned . . . and cried out and their cry for
      help . . . came up to God."
  (3) anticipates J's framework, God's "seeing" and "knowing"
    "and God saw the people of Israel and God knew . . ."

APPENDIX C: A QUESTION

What is the significance of the patterns of "appropriation" of the slaves' cry within the Exodus materials (and their counterparts throughout the Old Testament) for similar attempts at "appropriation" today?

(1) actual patterns of appropriation authoritative
     —J's cry for justice—resident alien in the U.S. courts
     —E's cry for liberation—peasants in Latin America
     —P's cry of pain in context of worship—distraught parishioner in the Presbyterian Church (U.S.A.)

(2) principle of "re-appropriation" alone authoritative
     need to constantly update our patterns of appropriation in light of changing social, political, and liturgical conditions

(3) must filter these patterns of appropriation through the New Testament's continuation of the cry in the life, death, and resurrection of Jesus Christ
     —J's cry for justice—Isa 42:1–4
     —E's cry for liberation—Isa 19:20
     —P's cry of pain—Isa 65:19

Bibliography

Albertz, Rainer. *Persönliche Frömmigkeit und offizielle Religion: Religionsinter-*
ner Pluralismus in Israel und Babylon. Calwer Theologische Monographien, Bd. 9. Stuttgart: Calwer Verlag, 1978. 302 pp.

————. " '*tr*, beten." In *Theologisches Handwörterbuch zum Alten Testament,*
2:385–86. Hrsq. von Ernst Jenni unter Mitarbeit von Claus Westermann.
München: Chr. Kaiser Verlag, 1971. 2 Bde.

————. "*s'q*, schreien." In *Theologisches Handwörterbuch zum Alten Testament,*
2:568–75. Hrsg. von Ernst Jenni unter Mitarbeit von Claus Westermann.
München: Chr. Kaiser Verlag, 1971. 2 Bde.

Anderson, A. A. *The Book of Psalms.* The New Century Bible Commentary.
Grand Rapids: Wm. B. Eerdmans Publishing Co., 1972. 2 vols.

Ap-Thomas, D. R. "Notes on Some Terms Relating to Prayer." *Vetus Testamen-*
tum 6 (1956) 225–41.

————. "Some Notes on the Old Testament Attitude to Prayer." *Scottish Journal*
of Theology 9 (1956) 422–29.

Balentine, Samuel E. *The Hidden God: The Hiding of the Face of God in the*
Old Testament. Oxford Theological Monographs. Oxford: University
Press, 1983. 202 pp.

————. "The Prophet as Intercessor: A Reassessment." *Journal of Biblical*
Literature 103 (1984) 161–73.

Barr, James. "An Aspect of Salvation in the Old Testament." In *Man and His*
Salvation: Studies in Memory of S. G. F. Brandon, pp. 39–92. Edited by
Eric J. Sharpe and John R. Hinnells. Manchester: University Press, 1973.
338 pp.

————. *Biblical Words for Time,* 2d ed. Studies in Biblical Theology, lst ser., no.
33. London: SCM Press, 1969. 221 pp.

————. "Common Sense and Biblical Language." *Biblica* 49 (1968) 377–87.

————. "Etymology and the Old Testament." In *Language and Meaning: Studies*
in Hebrew Language and Biblical Exegesis, pp. 1–28. Oudtestamentische
Studien, dl. 19. Leiden: E. J. Brill, 1974. 150 pp.

————. "The Image of God in the Book of Genesis: A Study of Terminology."
Bulletin of John Rylands Library 51 (1968–1969) 11–26.

————. "Semantics and Biblical Theology: A Contribution to the Discussion." In *Congress Volume,* pp. 11–29. Supplements to Vetus Testamentum, vol. 22. Leiden: E. J. Brill, 1972. 293 pp.

————. "Some Notes on the Covenant." In *Beiträge zur alttestamentlichen Theologie: Festschrift für Walter Zimmerli zum 70. Geburtstag,* pp. 23–38. Hrsg. von Herber Donner, Robert Hanhart, und Rudolf Smend. Göttingen: Vandenhoeck & Ruprecht, 1977. 580 pp.

Barth, Karl. *Church Dogmatics.* Edited by G. W. Bromiley and T. F. Torrance. Vol. 3/3, 4: *The Doctrine of Creation.* Edinburgh: T. & T. Clark, 1960–61. 4 vols.

Baumgartner, Walter. *Die Klagegedichte des Jeremia.* Beihefte zur Zeitschrift für die alttestamentliche Wissenschaft, Bd. 32. Giessen: Verlag von Alfred Töpelmann, 1917. 92 pp.

Begrich, J. "Das priesterliche Heilsorakel," *Zeitschrift für alttestamentliche Wissenschaft* 52 (1934) 81–92.

Bernhardt, Karl-Heinz. *Das Problem der altorientalischen Königs-Ideologie im Alten Testament: Unter besonder Berücksichtgung der Geschichte de Psalmenexegese dargestellt und kritisch Gewürdigt.* Supplements to Vetus Testamentum, vol. 8. Leiden: E. J. Brill, 1961. 351 pp.

Bird, Phyllis A. "Images of Women in the Old Testament." In *The Bible and Liberation: Political and Social Hermeneutics,* pp. 252–88. Edited by Norman K. Gottwald. Maryknoll: Orbis Books, 1983. 542 pp.

Blank, Sheldon H. "Some Observations Concerning Biblical Prayer." *Hebrew Union College Annual* 32 (1961) 75–90.

Blau, Joshua. *A Grammar of Biblical Hebrew.* Porta Linguarum Orientalium, n. S., no. 12. Wiesbaden: Otto Harrassowitz, 1976. 209 pp.

Boecker, Hans Jochen. *Redeformen des Rechtslebens im Alten Testament.* Wissenschaftliche Monographien zum Alten und Neuen Testament, Bd. 14. Neukirchen-Vluyn: Neukirchener Verlag, 1964. 182 pp.

Boesak, Allan Aubrey. *Black Theology, Black Power.* London: Mowbrays, 1976. 185 pp.

Brenner, Athalya. *Colour Terms in the Old Testament.* Journal for the Study of the Old Testament Supplement Series, no. 21. Sheffield: JSOT Press, 1982. 196 pp.

Bright, John. "Jeremiah's Complaints: Liturgy or Expressions of Personal Distress?" In *Proclamation and Presence: Old Testament Essays in Honor of Gwynne Hunton Davies,* pp. 189–214. Edited by John I. Durham and J. R. Porter. London: SCM Press, 1970. 315 pp.

Brown, Francis; Driver, S. R.; and Briggs, Charles A., eds. *A Hebrew and English Lexicon of the Old Testament.* Oxford: Clarendon Press, 1909. 1127 pp.

Brueggemann, Walter. "A Cosmic Sigh of Relinquishment." *Currents on Theology and Mission* 11 (February 1984) 5–20.

———. "From Hurt to Joy, From Death to Life." *Interpretation* 28 (January 1974) 3–19.

———. *Genesis: A Bible Commentary for Teaching and Preaching*. Interpretation. Atlanta: John Knox Press, 1982. 384 pp.

———. "Social Criticism and Social Vision in the Deuteronomic Formula of the Judges." In *Die Botschaft und die Boten: Festschrift für Hans Walter Wolff zum 70. Geburtstag*, pp. 101–14. Hrsg. von Jörg Jeremias und Lothar Perlitt. Neukirchen-Vluyn: Neukirchener Verlag, 1981. 426 pp.

———. "Trajectories in Old Testament Literature and the Sociology of Ancient Israel." In *The Bible and Liberation: Political and Social Hermeneutics*, pp. 307–333. Edited by Norman K. Gottwald. Maryknoll: Orbis Books, 1983. 542 pp.

Caird, G. B. *The Language and Imagery of the Bible*. Philadelphia: Westminster Press, 1980. 280 pp.

Carpenter, J. Estlin, and Harford-Battersby, G., eds. *The Hexateuch according to the Revised Version*. London: Longmans, Green, and Co., 1900. 2 vols.

Childs, Brevard S. *The Book of Exodus: A Critical, Theological Commentary*. The Old Testament Library. Philadelphia: Westminster Press, 1974. 659 pp.

———. *Introduction to the Old Testament as Scripture*. Philadelphia: Fortress Press, 1979. 688 pp.

———. *Memory and Tradition in Israel*. Studies in Biblical Theology. London: SCM Press, 1962. 96 pp.

De Fraine, J. *L'aspect religieux de la royauté Israélite: L'institution monarchique dans l'Ancien Testament et dans les textes Mésopotamiens*. Analecta Biblica, vol. 3. Rome: Pontifico Instituto Biblico, 1954. 425 pp.

Doller, Johannes. *Das Gebet im Alten Testament in religiongeschichtlicher Beleuchtung*. Theologische Studien der Österreichischen Leo-Gesellschaft, Bd. 21. Hildesheim: Verlag Dr. H. A. Gerstenberg, 1974. 107 pp.

Elliger, Karl. *Deuterojesaja*. Biblischer Kommentar Altes Testament, XI/1. Neukirchen-Vluyn: Neukirchener Verlag, 1978. 531 pp.

Elliger, K., and Rudolph, W., eds. *Biblica Hebraica Stuttgartensia*. Stuttgart: Deutsche Bibelstiftung, 1977. 1574 pp.

Even-Shoshan, Abraham, ed. *A New Concordance of the Bible*. Jerusalem: "Kiryat Sepher" Publishing House, 1980. 4 vols.

Farb, Peter. *Word Play: What Happens When People Talk*. New York: Alfred A. Knopf, 1974. 350 pp.

Fensham, F. Charles. "Widow, Orphan, and the Poor in Ancient Near Eastern Legal and Wisdom Literature." *Journal of Near Eastern Studies* 21 (April 1962) 129–39.

Fretheim, T. E. "Elohist." In *The Interpreter's Dictionary of the Bible, Supplementary Volume,* pp. 259–63. Nashville: Abingdon, 1976. 998 pp.

Fuchs, Ottmar. *Die Klage als Gebet: Eine theologische Besinnung am Beispiel des Psalms 22.* München: Kösel-Verlag, 1982. 372 pp.

Fuss, Werner. *Die deuteronomistische Pentateuchredaktion in Exodus 3–17.* Beiheft zur Zeitschrift für die alttestamentliche Wissenschaft, Bd. 126. Berlin: Walter de Gruyter, 1972. 406 pp.

Gamper, Arnold. *Gott als Richter in Mesopotamien und im Alten Testament: Zum Verständnis einer Gebetsbitte.* Innsbruck: Universitätsverlag Wagner, 1966. 256 pp.

Gemser, B. "The *rîb* — or Controversy — Pattern in Hebrew Mentality." In *Wisdom in Israel and in the Ancient Near East,* pp. 120–37. Supplements to Vetus Testamentum, vol. 3. Leiden: E. J. Brill, 1955. 301 pp.

Gerstenberger, Erhard S. *Der bittende Mensch: Bittritual und Klagelied des Einzelnen im Alten Testament.* Wissenschaftliche Monographien zum Alten und Neuen Testament, Bd. 51. Neukirchen-Vluyn: Neukirchener Verlag, 1980. 195 pp.

Gibson, Arthur. *Biblical Semantic Loqic: A Preliminary Analysis.* Oxford: Basil Blackwell, 1981. 244 pp.

Gonzalez, A. "Priere." In *Supplément au dictionnaire de la Bible,* 8:555–606. Paris: Letouzey & Ané, Editeurs, 1972. 1476 pp.

Greenberg, Moshe. *Biblical Prose Prayer: As a Window to the Popular Religion of Ancient Israel.* The Taubman Lectures in Jewish Studies, 6th ser. Berkeley: University of California Press, 1983. 66 pp.

Gruber, Mayer I. *Aspects of Nonverbal Communication in the Ancient Near East.* Studia Pohl, no. 12. Rome: Biblical Institute Press, 1980. 2 vols.

Gunkel, Hermann und Begrich, Joachim. *Einleitung in die Psalmen: Die Gattungen der religiössen Lyrik Israels.* Göttinger Handkommentar zum Alten Testament. Göttingen: Vandenhoeck & Ruprecht, 1933. 464 pp.

Guthrie, Harvey H., Jr. *Israel's Sacred Songs: A Study of Dominant Themes.* New York: Seabury Press, 1966. 241 pp.

Habel, Norman C. *Literary Criticism of the Old Testament.* Guides to Biblical Scholarship, Old Testament Series. Philadelphia: Fortress Press, 1971. 86 pp.

Hasel, G. "zā'aq." In *Theological Dictionary of the Old Testament*, 4:112–22. Edited by G. Johannes Botterweck and Helmar Ringgren. Translated by David E. Green. Grand Rapids: William B. Eerdmans Publishing Co., 1980. 493 pp.

Heiler, Friedrich. *Prayer: A Study in the History and Psychology of Religion*. Translated and edited by Samuel McComb. London: Oxford University Press, 1932. 376 pp.

Heller, Jan. "Das Gebet im Alten Testament: Begriffsanalyse." *Communio Viatorum* 19 (1976) 157–62.

Hermann, H. "Prayer in the Old Testament." In *Theological Dictionary of the New Testament*, 2:789–800. Edited by Gerhard Kittel. Translated and edited by Geoffrey W. Bromiley. Grand Rapids: William B. Eerdmans Publishing Company, 1964. 955 pp.

Holladay, William L. *A Concise Hebrew and Aramaic Lexicon of the Old Testament*. Grand Rapids: William B. Eerdmans Publishing Co., 1971. 425 pp.

Hyatt, J. P. *Exodus*. New Century Bible Commentary. Grand Rapids: William B. Eerdmans Publishing Co., 1971. 351 pp.

Irmscher, William F. *The Holt Guide to Enqlish: A Contemporary Handbook of Rhetoric, Language, and Literature*, 2d ed. New York: Holt, Rinehart, and Winston, 1972. 539 pp.

Jenks, Alan W. *The Elohist and North Israelite Traditions*. Society of Biblical Literature Monograph Series, no. 22. Missoula: Scholars Press, 1977. 147 pp.

Jeremias, Jörg. *Kultprophetie und Gerichtsverkündigung in der späten Königszeit Israels*. Wissenschaftliche Monographien zum Alten und Neuen Testament, Bd. 35. Neukirchen-Vluyn: Neukirchener Verlag, 1970. 214 pp.

Kaufman, Gordon D. *God the Problem*. Cambridge: Harvard University Press, 1972. 276 pp.

Kautzsch, E., ed. *Gesenius' Hebrew Grammar*. 2d English ed. Edited by A. E. Cowley. Oxford: Clarendon Press, 1910.

Keel, Othmar. *The Symbolism of the Biblical World: Ancient Near Eastern Iconography and the Book of Psalms*. Translated by Timothy J. Hallett. New York: Seabury Press, 1978. 422 pp.

Kirk, J. Andrew. *Liberation Theoloy: An Evangelical View from the Third World*. New Foundations Theological Library. Atlanta: John Knox Press, 1979. 246 pp.

Koch, Klaus. *The Growth of the Biblical Tradition: The Form-Critical Method*. Translated by S. M. Cupitt. New York: Charles Scribner's Sons, 1969. 233 pp.

Koehler, Ludwig and Baumgartner, Walter, eds. *Lexicon in Veteris Testamenti Libros.* Grand Rapids: William B. Eerdmans Publishing Co., 1953. 1138 pp.

Kraus, Hans-Joachim. *Worship in Israel: A Cultic History of the Old Testament.* Translated by Geoffrey Buswell. Richmond: John Knox Press, 1966.

Krinetzki, Leo. *Israels Gebet im Alten Testament.* Der Christ in der Welt, eine Enzyklopädie. 6. Reihe: Das Buch der Bucher, Bd. 5a. Aschaffenburg: Paul Pattloch Verlag, 1965. 111 pp.

Kushner, Harold S. *When Bad Things Happen to Good People.* New York: Avon, 1981. 149 pp.

Labuschagne, C. J. *"ntn,* geben." In *Theologisches Handwörterbuch zum Alten Testament,* 2:117–41. Hrsg. von Ernst Jenni unter Mitarbeit von Claus Westermann. München: Chr. Kaiser Verlag, 1971. 2 Bde.

———. *"qr',* rufen." In *Theologisches Handwörterbuch zum Alten Testament,* 2:666–74. Hrsg. von Ernst Jenni unter Mitarbeit von Claus Westermann. München: Chr. Kaiser Verlag, 1971. 2 Bde.

Longacre, R. E. *An Anatomy of Speech Notions.* PdR Press Publications in Tagmemics, no. 3. Lisse: Peter de Ridder Press, 1976. 394 pp.

Lyons, John. *Introduction to Theoretical Linguistics.* Cambridge: University Press, 1968. 519 pp.

Macholz, Georg Christian. "Die Stellung des Königs in der israelitischen Gerichtsverfassung." *Zeitschrift für die alttestamentliche Wissenschaft* 84 (1972) 157–82.

McKane, William. *Proverbs: A New Approach.* The Old Testament Library. Philadelphia: Westminster Press, 1970. 670 pp.

MacLaurin, E. C. B. *The Hebrew Theocracy in the Tenth to the Sixth Centuries B.C.: An Analysis of the Books of Judges, Samuel, and Kings.* London: Angus & Robertson, 1959. 139 pp.

Mandelkern, Solomon. *Veteris Testamenti Concordantiae Hebraicae atque Chaldaicae.* Berlin: F. Margolin, 1925.

Marcus, Ralph. "The 'Plain Meaning' of Isaiah 42:1–4." *The Harvard Theological Review* 30 (1937) 249–59.

Mayes, A. D. H. *The Story of Israel between Settlement and Exile: A Redactional Study of the Deuteronomistic History.* London: SCM Press, 1983. 202 pp.

Mays, James Luther. *Hosea: A Commentary.* The Old Testament Library. London: SCM Press, 1969. 190 pp.

———. *Micah: A Commentary.* The Old Testament Library. Philadelphia: Westminster Press, 1976. 169 pp.

Meyer, D. Rudolf. *Hebräische Grammatik,* Dritte Aufl. Berlin: Walter de Gruyter, 1972. 4 Bde.

Meyers, Carol L. "The Roots of Restriction: Women in Early Israel." In *The Bible and Liberation: Political and Social Hermeneutics*, pp. 289-306. Edited by Norman K. Gottwald. Maryknoll: Orbis Books, 1983. 542 pp.

Miller, Patrick D., Jr. *The Divine Warrior in Early Israel*. Harvard Semitic Monographs, vol 5. Cambridge: Harvard University Press, 1973. 279 pp.

————. "Trouble and Woe: Interpreting the Biblical Laments." *Interpretation* 37 (January 1983) 32-45.

Miranda, Jose Porfirio. *Marx and the Bible: A Critique of the Philosophy of Oppression*. Maryknoll: Orbis Books, 1974. 338 pp.

Morris, William, ed. *The American Heritage Dictionary of the English Language*. Boston: Houghton Mifflin Co., 1976. 1950 pp.

Mowinckel, Sigmund. *The Psalms in Israel's Worship*. Translated by D. R. Ap-Thomas. Nashville: Abingdon, 1962. 2 vols.

Nielson, Kirsten. *Yahweh as Prosecutor and Judge: An Investigation of the Prophetic Lawsuit (Rib Pattern)*. Journal for the Study of the Old Testament Supplement Series, no. 9. Sheffield: JSOT, 1978. 104 pp.

Noth, Martin. *Exodus: A Commentary*. The Old Testament Library. Philadelphia: Westminster Press, 1962. 283 pp.

Pedersen, Johannes. *Israel: Its Life and Culture*. London: Oxford University Press, 1926. 4 vols. in 2.

Plastaras, James. *The God of Exodus: The Theology of the Exodus Narratives*. Milwaukee: Bruce Publishing Co., 1966. 342 pp.

Pritchard, James B., ed. *Ancient Near Eastern Texts Relating to the Old Testament*. 3d ed. with Supplement. Princeton: Princeton University Press, 1969. 710 pp.

Rad, Gerhard von. *Genesis: A Commentary*. 2d ed. Translated by John H. Marks. The Old Testament Library. Philadelphia: Westminster Press, 1972. 440 pp.

————. *Old Testament Theology*. Translated by D. M. G. Stalker. New York: Harper & Row, Publishers, 1962. 2 vols.

Richter, Wolfgang. *Die Bearbeitungen des "Retterbuches" in der deuteronomischen Epoche*. Bonner Biblische Beiträge, Bd. 21. Bonn: Peter Haustein Verlag, 1964. 148 pp.

Rogers, M. G. "The Book of Judges." In *The Interpreter's Dictionary of the Bible, Supplementary Volume*, pp. 509-514. Nashville: Abingdon, 1976. 998 pp.

Sawyer, John F. A. *Semantics in Biblical Research: New Methods of Defining Hebrew Words for Salvation*. Studies in Biblical Theology, 2d ser., no. 24. London: SCM Press, 1972. 146 pp.

Schmid, Hans Heinrich. *Gerechtigkeit als Weltordnung: Hintergrund und Geschichte des alttestamentlichen Gerechtigkeitsbegriffes.* Beiträge zur historischen Theologie, Bd. 40. Tübingen: J. C. B. Mohr, 1968. 203 pp.

————. *Der sogenannte Jahwist: Beobachtungen und Fragen zur Pentateuchforschung.* Zürich: Theologischer Verlag, 1976. 194 pp.

Schmidt, Werner H. *"dābhar."* In *Theological Dictionary of the Old Testament,* 3:94-125. Edited by G. Johannes Betterweck und Helmer Ringgren. Translated by John T. Willis and Geoffrey W. Bromiley. Grand Rapids: William B. Eerdmans Publishing Co., 1978. 463 pp.

————. *Exodus.* Biblischer Kommentar Altes Testament, Bd. II/2. Neukirchen-Vluyn: Neukirchener Verlag, 1977. pp. 81-160 [sic]

Seeligmann, I. L. "Zur Terminologie für das Gerichtsverfahren im Wortschatz des biblischen Hebräische." In *Hebräische Wortforschung: Festschrift zum 80. Geburtstag von Walter Baumgartner,* pp. 251-78. Supplements to Vetus Testamentum, vol. 16. Leiden: E. J. Brill, 1967.

Seibert, Ilse. *Women in Ancient Near East.* Translated by Marianne Herzfeld. Leipzig: Edition Leipzig, 1974. 66 pp.

Silva, Moisés. *Biblical Words and Their Meaning: An Introduction to Lexical Semantics.* Grand Rapids: Zondervan Publishing House, 1983. 201 pp.

Soggin, J. Alberta. *Judges: A Commentary.* Translated by John Bowden. The Old Testament Library. Philadelphia: Westminster Press, 1981. 305 pp.

"Sojourners Book Service." Sojourners, October 1984, pp. 32-33.

Stähli, H.-P. *"pll hitp., beten."* In *Theologisches Handwörterbuch zum alten Testament,* 2:427-432. Hrsg. von Ernst Jenni unter Mitarbeit von Claus Westermann. München: Chr. Kaiser Verlag, 1971. 2 Bde.

Stolz, F. *"nśʾ, aufheben, tragen."* In *Theologisches Handwörterbuch zum Alten Testament,* 2:109-117. Hrsg. von Ernst Jenni unter Mitarbeit von Claus Westermann. München: Chr. Kaiser Verlag, 1971. 2 Bde.

Ullmann, Stephen. *Semantics: An Introduction to the Science of Meaning.* New York: Barnes & Noble, 1962. 278 pp.

Vaux, Roland de. *Ancient Israel.* New York: McGraw-Hill Book Co., 1961. 2 vols.

Wagner, S. *"ʾāmar."* In *Theological Dictionary of the Old Testament.* 2d ed., 1:328-45. Edited by G. Johannes Botterweck and Helmer Ringgren. Translated by John T. Willis. Grand Rapids: William B. Eerdmans Publishing Co., 1977. 479 pp.

Weimar, Peter. *Die Berufung des Mose: Literaturwissenschaftliche Analyse von Exodus 2.23-5.5.* Orbis Biblicus et Orientalis, Bd. 32. Göttingen: Vandenhoeck & Ruprecht, 1980. 399 pp.

Weingreen, J. *A Practical Grammar for Classical Hebrew,* 2d ed. Oxford: Clarendon Press, 1959.